Rumi
and the
Whirling Dervishes

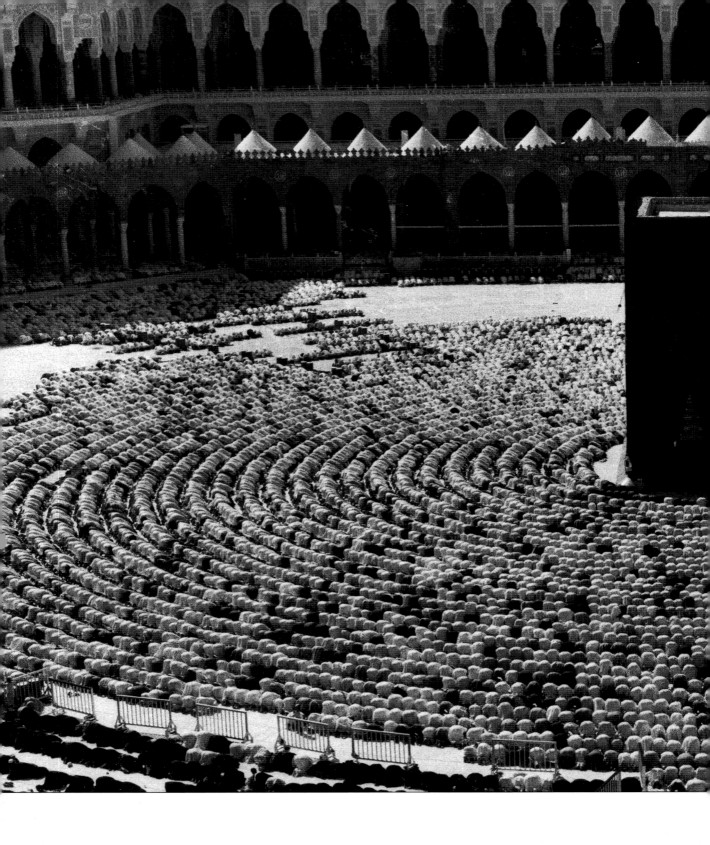

Just as the *hajjis* (pilgrims) chant supplications and exclaim *Allahu Akbar* while performing their circum-ambulation of the revered *Ka'ba,* just as the angels revolve around their gatherings for learning and remembrance, so do the lovers and dervishes who follow the Sufi orders make circling movements while reciting aloud the Divine Names *Hayy, Allah, Qayyum, Da'im, Ahad, Samad* (Ever-Living, Allah, Self-Existent, Everlasting, One, Eternal).

Rumi
and the
Whirling Dervishes

Being an account of the Sufi order
known as the Mevlevis
and its founder the poet and mystic
Mevlana Jalalu'ddin Rumi

by Shems Friedlander
Music section by Nezih Uzel
Foreword by Annemarie Schimmel
Preface by Seyyed Hossein Nasr

PARABOLA BOOKS
New York

Book design by Shems Friedlander

First PARABOLA Edition

Grateful acknowledgement is given to the following for permission to quote: George Allen and Unwin, London, for excerpts from *Rumi, Poet and Mystic,* translated by R. A. Nicholson, copyright 1964. Also, acknowledgement to the following from which excerpts have been taken: *Classical Persian Literature* by Al-Ghazzali, translated by A. J. Arberry, George Allen and Unwin, London, 1958; *Al-Ghazzali the Mystic* translated by Margaret Smith, Luzac & Co., London, 1944; *Memoirs of Saints* by Farid Al-Din Attar, translated by Dr. B. Behari, Sh. Muhammad Ashraf, Lahore, Pakistan, 1961; *Sufis of Andalusia* by Ibn 'Arabi, translated by R. W. J. Austin, George Allen and Unwin, London, 1971; *The Sufi Message* by Hazrat Inayat Khan, Barrie and Rockliff, London; *Ikwan Al-Safa Rasai'l, An Introduction to Islamic Cosmological Doctrines* by Seyyed Hossein Nasr, Belknap Press, Cambridge, Mass., 1964; *Divani Shamsi Tabriz* by Rumi, translated by R. A. Nicholson, The Rainbow Bridge, San Francisco, 1973; *Mathnawi* by Rumi, translated by R. A. Nicholson, Luzac & Co., London, 1925-40; *Rubaiyat* by Rumi, translated by A. J. Arberry, Emery Walker, London, 1949; *Naam or Word* by Kirpal Singh, Ruhani Satsang, Delhi, 1972; *Signs of the Unseen* by Rumi, translated by W. M. Thackston, Jr., Shambhala, Boston, 1999; *The Unveiling of Love* by Sheikh Muzaffer Ozak Al-Jerrahi, Inner Traditions, New York, 1981.

I would like to thank Talat Sait Halman, Professor of Turkish Studies at Princeton University, The British Museum, and the Tourist Association of Konya, Turkey.

Published by PARABOLA Books
     656 Broadway
     New York, NY 10012
     www.parabola.org

PARABOLA Books are published by the Society for the Study of Myth and Tradition, a not-for-profit organization devoted to the dissemination and exploration of materials relating to myth, symbol, ritual, and art of the great religious traditions. The Society also publishes PARABOLA, The Magazine of Myth, Tradition, and the Search for Meaning.

Library of Congress Cataloging-in-Publication Data
Friedlander, Shems.
    [Whirling dervishes]
    Rumi and the whirling dervishes / by Shems Friedlander ; foreword by Annemarie Schimmel.
        p. cm.
    Previously published as: The whirling dervishes.
    Includes bibliographical references.
    ISBN 0-930407-59-0 (pbk. : alk. paper)
    1. Jalal al-Din Rumi, Maulana, 1207–1273. 2. Mevleviyeh. 3. Mysticism--History--
    Middle Ages, 600–1500. 4. Sufism--History. I. Title.
BP189.7.M42 F76 2003
297.4'82'09--dc21

                                                                                    2002193040

10 9 8 7 6 5 4 3 2 1

The paper used in this publication meets the minimum requirements of the American National Standard for Permanence of Paper for Printed Library Materials Z39.48–1984.

Printed in China.

CONTENTS

For Nuri, Adam, and Sara

To the teaching of Mevlana
May it find its way to every heart.

Come, come whoever you are,
An unbeliever, a fire-worshipper, come.
Our covenant is not of desperation.
Even if you have broken your vows a hundred times,
Come, come again.

Mevlana Jalalu'ddin Rumi
September 30, 1207–December 17, 1273

If you are possessed of discernment joined
with knowledge, seek the company of the
dervishes and become one with them.
Love for the dervishes is the key which opens
the door to Paradise. The dervish's garment is
nothing but a patched robe, and he is not led
astray by earthly desires and passions.

Farid al-din 'Attar

Foreword

Dance is the movement of those who try to shed their earth-bound bodily garb to leave the material center of gravitation and to be drawn into a loftier, spiritual world; of those who leave the realm of confused everyday movements to whirl around the spiritual Sun like dust motes, like atoms; of those who join the movement of the blessed paradise, which is captured so beautifully in Fra Angelico's paintings.

In many ancient civilizations, dance was an offering to the deities who might enjoy the harmonious movements of men and women. But it is also an offering of one's own self: does not the moth circumambulate the candle, dancing, as it were, to immolate itself in the end in the flame which is enchanting light and consuming fire, representative of Divine Beauty and Majesty?

Dance was practiced by the Sufis from early days; in the late ninth century the first *semahanes* were founded–houses where the Sufis could relax somewhat from their intense spiritual work and harsh asceticism. Soon, many onlookers considered the whirling dance an essential part of Sufism–very much to the chagrin of the "sober" Sufis, let alone the orthodox lawyers. However, the only brotherhood in which the whirling was ever institutionalized as part of the ritual was the *Mevleviyya,* for Mevlana Rumi himself sang his immortal verses while whirling, enthralled by passionate longing for his friend Shams, the "Sun of Tabriz," who opened to him the way to immediate experience of the Divine Beloved.

Love, however, means to die to one's self and to be revived in the Beloved, and as much as the whirling dance can be interpreted as the dance

of everything created around the central Sun of Divine Love, it also means to re-enact death and resurrection: the dervishes cast off their black coats, symbols of earthly life, and appear in their unfolding white gowns–garb of immorality–like moths in enraptured and yet carefully measured dance, burning, it seems, in the flames of transfiguring Love.

Whoever has seen the ritual dance of the Mevlevis–especially in former times when some of the old dervishes were still alive, who had been "cooked" during the initial education that lasted for a thousand and one days–whoever has experienced this, knows how correctly the German poet Friedrich Ruckert understood this secret when he sang in his *ghazals* devoted to Mevlana Rumi's spirit in 1819 about the dance which he had never seen:

> He who knows the whirling's power,
>   lives in GOD
> For he knows how Love is slaying–
>   Allah Hu!
> Wer die Kraft des Reigens kennet,
>   Lebt in Gott,
> Denn er weiss, wie Liebe töte–
>   Allah Hu!

Annemarie Schimmel
Cambridge, Massachusetts

Preface

The foremost Sufi poet of the Persian language–and, according to many, of any language–Jalalu'ddin Rumi, left behind two monumental poetic works, the *Mathnawi*, and the *Diwan-i Kabir* or *Diwan-i Shams*, along with a number of shorter prose writings and some quatrains. The *Mathnawi* is like the ocean of gnosis and illuminative knowledge into which the seeker must dive deeply in order to discover the countless pearls of wisdom contained therein. The *Diwan-i Shams*, dedicated to the mysterious figure of Shams al-Din Tabrizi, who created flames of consuming love in the soul of Rumi, is an ecstatic work that burns through its fire the separative consciousness of the inspired reader and induces transformative love in his or her being. The two works mark the wedding between consuming love and illuminative knowledge that is central to the spiritual heritage of Mawlana (Mevlana in Turkish).

Yet despite the extreme significance of these works, which have influenced numerous generations of Persians, Turks, Indian Muslims and others during the past seven centuries and many Westerners today, these and other writings of Rumi are not the only heritage that he left behind. Nor are they the only keys to the understanding of the spiritual universe of the great master of Sufism buried in Konya. There are also the Sufi practices that need to be considered. Rumi founded a new Sufi order, systematized later by his son and named after the father as the Mawlawiyyah or Mevlevi Order. This order dominated the spiritual life of Turkey and many other parts of the Ottoman world up to the beginning of the twentieth century and still survives in Turkey despite having been banned there in the 1920s. Rumi received as inspiration from Heaven the sacred dance that has made the order so famous and that even attracted the attention of early European travelers, who referred to the Mevlevis as whirling dervishes. Rumi also brought the extensive use of music to his order and over the centuries the Mevlevi Order has played a major role in the creation and transmission of traditional Turkish music. Other Sufi orders have *sama'* or *sema* comprised of both bodily movements and music. Some, such as the Chishstiyyah of India, pay special attention to the use of music in their gatherings and like the Mevlevis have musicians associated with their Sufi centers. But there is no Sufi order in Islam in which both music and dance, considered as sacred activities that draw the soul to God, have been so elaborately formulated as in the Mevlevi Order.

The special value of the present volume is that it makes available to the Western reader through both images and words this central aspect of the heritage of Rumi, which is still a living reality, having been perpetuated generation after generation by those dervishes who have been initiated into the Mevlevi Order and who have meticulously preserved and continued the sema. Moreover, the author, who is himself associated with Sufism and has traveled extensively in Turkey, has been able to present to the reader of this work visual depictions and descriptions of the sema that are marked by authenticity, and that in fact were preserved until now only for those within the Order.

Today Rumi has become very famous in America but the cost of this fame has often been the dilution of the meaning of his words and the severance of his message from the Islamic tradition to which he belonged with his whole being. It is as if Dante were to be translated very approximately into Arabic and presented as a "universal poet," which he of course is, but without any reference to Christianity, without which Dante would not be Dante. The same truth holds for Rumi, who represents one of the greatest flowerings of Islamic spirituality, a tradition whose roots are sunk deeply in the Koran and whose prototype is to be found in the Prophet of Islam. The present book makes this reality abundantly clear and helps to prevent Rumi from becoming seen as a "universal" New Age poet without grounding in a distinct revelation and within a traditional framework.

Shems Friedlander must be congratulated in composing a book that reflects the authentic Mevlevi tradition and emphasizes the concrete practices and spiritual attitudes of the Order. He has made it possible for the general public to understand better its ambience and especially the sema or spiritual concert and sacred dance which provided the immediate context for the composition of much of Rumi's poetry, a poetry which because of the depth of its meaning is also of the greatest universal import today. May this book make clearer to the Western public the vast contours as well as content of the spiritual universe of Jalalu'ddin Rumi, one of the foremost saints of Sufism and one of the greatest metaphysical and mystical poets the world has ever known.

Seyyed Hossein Nasr
January 2003

Introduction

Dust on the Path of Muhammad

> I am a bird of the heavenly garden
> I belong not to the earthly sphere,
> They have made for two or three days
> A cage of my body.

> —Mevlana Jalalu'ddin Rumi

For over 700 years, men in black cloaks have performed a whirling dance in a continual remembrance of their Creator. The Sufi poet and mystic Jalalu'ddin Rumi began the whirling dance and the dervish order known as the Mevlevis. Since his passing in 1273 the Mevlevis have made their *zikr* in a whirling fashion, which was stylized by Rumi's son Sultan Veled on the basis of the movements established by his father.

In 1924, with the overthrow of the Ottoman Empire, the Turn was interrupted for over 25 years. Then a small group of dervishes convinced the local government in Konya that it would be harmless to introduce the Turn "as a historical tradition" to the new culture of Turkey. UNESCO invited the Mevlevis to Paris in 1964. In this, their first European trip, Selman Tuzon and Suleyman Loras sat on the Sheikh's red post as nine *semazen* turned to the music of several dervish musicians. This event signaled the beginning of a widespread interest in the West about the remarkable works of Rumi.

Since then the sema has been done in Konya to honor the *sheb-i arus*, the Wedding Night of Jalalu'ddin Rumi, (the night of his passing).

The turners pass the post and bow to the Sheikh. Their tall felt hats, representing their own tombstones, are tightly pulled over their ears so as not to fly off during the spin. In the Sultan Veled Walk they trail the Sheikh around the semahane still wearing the black cloak, which symbolizes the grave, the box of their actions. Before they begin to whirl, each lets fall the black cloak and, like a fledgling bird, unfolds and stretches out his arms as the long white *tennure,* the shroud of their future, engraves a circle in the air. With each turn they invoke the Name of Allah, and perhaps for a moment experience their death before dying.

When the seed of love is planted in the heart of a believer, only Allah knows where it will bear fruit. The sema is like a spiritual field where one can plant seeds of faith.

A person without faith is like a man who arrives at the marketplace after dark. In the darkness, this man cannot tell what he is buying. There are all kinds of people among the sellers. He pays his money and stuffs whatever they give him into his sack. He does not examine what he is getting. That man has paid his money, but he has no idea what he bought. Back home, he empties his sack. He thought he had bought a rope, but finds he has a snake. The honey proves to be tar. The meat is a stinking carcass. All his money has been wasted, and he has bought himself a heap of trouble into the bargain. The human being entering this world is like a man going to market in the dark.

Listen to the words of the Sufi poet:

> To market we came
> From our mother's womb,
> We bought a shroud,
> Then back to the tomb.

And as Jalalu'ddin Rumi aptly expresses his attitude with these lines:

> I am the slave of the Koran
> While I still have life.
> I am the dust on the path of Muhammad,
> The Chosen One.
> If anyone interprets my words
> In any other way,
> I deplore that person,
> And I deplore his words.

—Shems Friedlander

The entire Koran is
embroidered on this
Ottoman shirt.

The Sufi

There was a tradesman in a small village in the East who sat on his knees in his little shop, and with his left hand pulled a strand of wool from the bale above his head. He twirled the wool into a thicker strand and passed it to his right hand as it came before his body. The right hand wound the wool around a large spindle. This was a continuous motion on the part of the old man, who each time his right hand spindled the wool, inaudibly said *"la illaha illa 'llah."* There could be no uneven movement or the wool would break and he would have to tie a knot and begin again. The old man had to be present to every moment or he would break the wool. This is awareness. This is life. *Sufi* means awareness in life, awareness on a higher plane than that on which we normally live.

He was a simple man and taught his sons his trade.

The Persian word *darwish* (literally, the sill of the door) is accepted in Arabic and Turkish (*dervish*) to describe the Sufi, who is the one at the door to enlightenment.

Some say the label *Sufi* (in Arabic *suf* means wool) grew from the wool cloaks worn by these holy beings. Others like to think that its origin is from the Greek word *sophos,* which means wisdom.

**Top: Detail of an early 17th-century Mughal painting of a poet in contemplation.
Above: Persian miniature of a dervish seated in meditation.**

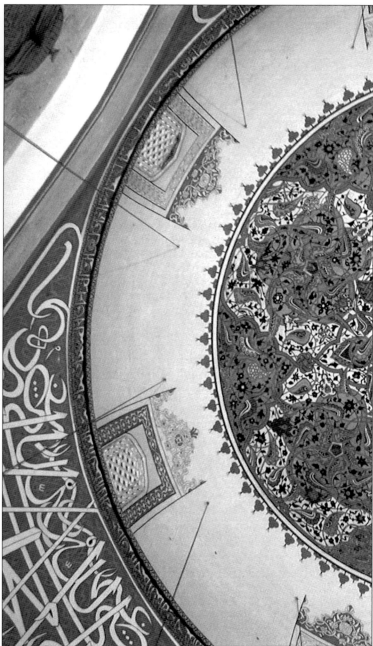

Above: Two views of the ceiling in the Mevlevi semahane, now part of the Museum in Konya. In the center of the triangle on the left is the name of the Prophet Muhammad repeated as a mirror image.
Left: Detail of a door in the Konya Mevlevi museum.

Appear as you are.
Be as you appear.

–Rumi

Neutralizing the Earth's Glue

Everything in the world is invisible except that which we make semi-visible. By the introduction of awareness, all things can become visible. The aim of the dervish is to open the eyes of the heart and see infinity in eternity. His goal is to loosen himself from the earth's glue which binds him and become one with God, to become a channel for His Light, and enter the realm of no boundaries.

Why is man interested in the magic flying carpet? Where does he think it will carry him? To a land of fantasy or to a place outside of himself where each being has inner peace and freedom? The mystic Rabia was in her house one day when her friend said, "Come out and behold what God has made." Rabia answered, "Come in and behold the Maker."

In the *Mathnawi,* Jalalu'ddin Rumi said:

A page from an early Koran in the Istanbul Museum.

> In a fair orchard, full of trees and fruit
> And vines and greenery, a Sufi sat with
> Eyes closed, his head upon his knees,
> Sunk deep in meditation, mystical.
> "Why," asked another, "dost thou not behold
> These signs of God the Merciful displayed
> Around thee, which He bids us contemplate?"
> "The signs," he answered, "I behold within;
> Without is naught but symbols of the Signs."

The experience of looking within, uncovering the buried treasure on which we sleep and living in the moment, has been transmitted through the chain of Sufism. The *Naqshibendi* Sheikh Necmeddin said:

> When you are everywhere, you are nowhere.
> When you are somewhere, you are everywhere.

Sheikh Muzaffer of the *Halveti* (secluded) dervishes of Istanbul describes the weaving of the magic flying carpet. "We do zikr to open the eyes of our heart. It is important to see with your heart's eyes, not with the eyes in your head. If you see through your heart you will know all men, all things; you will see like a telescope with a wide lens. If you only see with the eyes in your head you are no different from an animal. An animal has a head, eyes, nose, muscle, skin, ears; you are alike except that you can see through your heart's eyes. When you see with the eyes of your heart, all space opens for you."

Man is the magic flying carpet, and the ability to fly, to rise above all things, completes the weaving process of the carpet. It is the esoteric meaning of Jesus walking on the water and the mythical horse Buraq (breath) which flew the Prophet Muhammad from Madinah to Jerusalem and then to heaven.

In Hindu mythology, the giant bird Garuda (breath) carried the Gods to Heaven. By becoming aware of breath, man can virtually ride on his own breath and rise above earthly situations. Rumi once remarked, "A bird that flies upward does not reach the skies, yet it rises far above the rooftops and so escapes."

The dervish experiences a similar freedom. He may not become the "perfect man," but he gains a majestic quality in life that neutralizes the earth's glue, freeing him from worldly cares and anxieties.

A dervish tells the story of his sheikh, a man famous for his love of God, who used to spread his cloak on a lake adjoining the *tekke*. Seated upon it, he was carried wherever he liked. The Sufi poet Sa'di relates in his *Bustan* the tale of the dervish who crossed a river on his prayer carpet because he could not pay the ferryman's fee.

The method of the Sufis is zikr, the repetition of "la illaha illa'llah" (there is no god but God). There are some Sufis who only repeat "Allah" because they know man can die at any moment, and they want only the name of God on their lips and in their hearts. All Sufi orders perform zikr. The manner in which zikr is performed is the essential difference in the various orders. Zikr opens the door to the spiritual world which can also be opened by a gift from Allah.

Sufism is for human beings. It brings to humanity the culture of mankind. The Sufi leads a rhythmic life. In the Koran it is written:

> "Men whom neither trading nor selling diverts
> from the remembrance of God (zikr)..."

Out of the being of Mevlana Jalalu'ddin Rumi grew one of the most important and visually exciting dervish orders: the Mevlevis or Whirling Dervishes. At one point in his life, after meeting the wandering dervish, the man in rags, Shams Tabriz, Rumi went through a metamorphosis that shifted his center of manifestation from mind to heart. Although very little was known of Shams, there is no doubt that he belonged to a group which knew how to interiorize oneself, thereby reaching the place of the *Kalam-i-qadim*, the ancient word. He described this as a place where:

There comes a Sound, from neither within nor without,
From neither right nor left, from neither behind nor in front,
From neither below nor above, from neither East nor West,
Nor is it of the elements: water, air, fire, earth, and the like.
From where then? It is from that place thou art in search of;
Turn ye toward the place wherefrom the Lord makes His appearance.
From where a restless fish out of water gets water to live in,
From the place where the prophet Moses saw the divine Light,
From the place where the fruits get their ripening influence,
From the place where the stones get transmuted to gems,
From the place to which even an infidel turns in distress,
From the place to which all men turn when they find this world
      a veil of tears.
It is not given to us to describe such a blessed place;
It is a place where even the heretics would leave off their heresies.

Detail of an illustration of the Ka'ba in Makkah from a 19th-century Turkish miniature.

The Sufi master Hazrat Inayat Khan says of Shams, "Shams of Tabriz was an example of a soul who had fully attained God-consciousness, who had arrived at a stage where even mentioning the name of God limited his power as name limits God. And his life proved that the realization of truth stands above words. People say he experienced ecstasy. But I say he himself was ecstasy. And to the seekers of truth, even today, his words move to ecstasy."

The *Diwan-i Shamsi Tabriz,* containing 2,500 mystical odes, is an outpouring of feelings and thoughts that describes the natural state of man, a state that is unfamiliar to ordinary life. It is so different in character and style from Rumi's *Mathnawi* that one wonders whether Shams was not the author.

Within Rumi was the complete oneness of life. He was the living example of a man thoroughly in life. He was a father, husband, and university professor, and he merged all these aspects into a unified existence, linking all of his life with the thought of God and the practices toward humanity that this thought manifests. He "broke through to the Oneness," and solved the problem of "seeing One with two eyes."

Although there were men who lived within the principles of Sufism well before they were so labeled, the Sufi orders we know of today had their foundations with the Prophet Muhammad.

In the autumn of A.D. 622 Muhammad departed from his native Makkah and journeyed 200 miles north to Madinah where the structure of Islam was becoming more manifest. The Muslims accept this date, the day of "Emigration" (*Hijra*), as the beginning of the era known as Islam. The holy doctrine of Islam is the Koran, which was revealed by the angel Gabriel to Muhammad, over a period of twenty-three years, in the form of *suras* (chapters) that often pertained to specific instances in his life. All suras of the Koran begin with the words: *"Bismi'llah ir-rahman ir-rahim"* (In the Name of God, the Compassionate One, the Merciful), except sura *at-Tauba*. The opening sura of the Koran is a prayer called the *Fatihah*, which is said by all Muslims during their daily prayers:

> Praise to God, the Lord of the worlds,
> The Compassionate, the Merciful,
> The King of the day of Judgment.
> It is Thee whom we adore and it is with
> Thee we seek refuge.
> Lead us on the straight way,
> The way of those on whom is Thy grace,
> Not (that of) those who suffer Thy wrath,
>   nor of those who stray.

Sufism (*Tasawwuf*) is the esoteric aspect of Islam. Its purpose is to convey direct knowledge of the eternal. The Sufis impart knowledge through a *silsilah* (chain) of beings that goes back to the Prophet Muhammad. Much of the knowledge was never written down but passed on orally, and many aspects of Sufism find their origin in the Koran.

There are different Sufi orders or paths (*tariqa*) in which the aspirant receives initiation by means of *bayah,* a covenant of allegiance to a sheikh. The repetition of a zikr that includes the "taking of hand" is part of the ceremony. In the Koran, it is written:

> Those who swear fidelity to thee
> swear fidelity in truth to God;
> the hand of God is over their hands.
> Whoever violates his oath,
> violates it to his own hurt;
> whoever fulfills his promise to God,
> God will surely give him a great reward.

To the Sufi, the body is the Temple of God, or, as Muhyi-d-Din Ibn 'Arabi says, it is "the ark where dwells the Peace of the Lord." Training in the dervish tekke is a process of cleansing the ark. In his thirteenth-century *Rose Garden of Mystery* Mahmud Shabistari said:

> Go sweep out the chamber of your heart.
> Make it ready to be the dwelling place of the Beloved.
> When you depart out He will enter it.
> In you, void of yourself, will
> He display His beauties.

The Koran says that when Moses reached the Burning Bush he was called by name: "O Moses! Verily I am thy Lord. Take off thy sandals. Verily thou art in the holy Valley of Tuwa."

Moses experienced what the Sufis call *fana*, complete annihilation in the Truth of Certainty, followed by *baqa*, the eternal subsistence in God. His sandals represented his separation from the Creator. When the dervish enters the mosque or tekke, he removes his shoes. He leaves his worldly attachments outside and then enters the House of God or room of celestial sounds.

Mansur al Hallaj, a disciple of the great Sufi Sheikh Junaid of Baghdad, later said: "When Truth has overwhelmed a human heart, it empties it of all that is not Truth. When God loves a being, He kills everything that is not Him."

"Enough of phrases, conceit, and metaphors, I want burning, burning, burning." These words of Jalalu'ddin Rumi excite the very essence of our being, reflecting the man Moses, barefoot, his body vibrating with light from the Divine Light.

When the great woman Sufi saint Rabia of Basra made the *hajj* (pilgrimage to Makkah) and saw the *Ka'ba,* she said, "I see only bricks and a house of stone; what do they profit me? 'Tis Thou that I want."

Al-Ghazzali has written: "There is a great difficulty in knowing God because His brightness is too much for the heart of man to bear. Man knows the extraordinary brightness of the sun, which reveals all things, yet if the earth did not revolve around the sun causing night, or if shade did not veil it, no one would know that light exists. He is hidden by His brightness." In the *Mathnawi* Rumi is attracted by the meaning of light:

> 'Tis light makes color visible; at night
> Red, green, and russet vanish from thy sight.
> So too the light by darkness is made known.
> All hid things by their contraries are shown.

A late 19th-century water-color from a book on Ottoman costume.

A *hadith* says, "I was a hidden treasure and I wanted to be known, so I created the world in order that I may be known." First there is knowledge–not the knowledge of the head, but knowledge in the heart. One must become educated by one's heart to the things that cannot be understood intellectually. If we transpose the quote, a secret is revealed:

> Known, loved, Him, I.

Love is a cyclic situation. First He loved man, so that man could love Him. Man is His own image.

> I created man in my own image,
> and unto him I insufflated of my own spirit.

Therefore, man alone of all creation is capable of being the complete image. This is the purpose of creation–to complete the love affair, the first lover being Him.

He said to David, "Oh David, if you only knew how much my love is more than theirs for me."

True love, the love which Mevlana expounds, is love with knowledge; it is metaphysical love.

"My secret," said Mevlana, "is not far from my plaint, but ear and eye lack the light. Body is not veiled from soul, nor soul from body, yet none is permitted to see the soul." In the *Mathnawi,* Mevlana states, "Even the earth and water and fire which seem to us as dead things, before God they are living beings, obedient to His Will."

More recently, Sheikh Muzaffer of the Halveti dervishes said, "Philosophy is finished. Now is the time for love. God wants love."

Without knowledge love loses its direction. It becomes diversified, split, a wasteland, like water losing itself in the desert. The love of the Sufi has to be directed to Him. This is only possible with knowledge of Him.

God is man. Man is no other than God. But man is not God. The Sufis say: "If you seek Him, you will never find Him. But if you do not seek Him, He will not reveal Himself to you."

To his circle of listeners Rumi said: "He created Adam in His own image, that is in the image of His laws. All of His laws are visible in His creatures because they are all 'shadows of God,' and a shadow resembles the person who cast it. If you spread your fingers, your shadow will do so too. If you bow down, your shadow will do so too. Therefore people who are searching are looking for something to seek, something to love, for they want to be loving and humble before Him, enemies to His enemies and friends to His friends. These are all laws and attributes of God that appear in the shadow. The shadow we cast is unaware of us, but we are aware of it.

"However, in relation to God's knowledge, our awareness counts for no more than unawareness. Not everything in a person is contained in his shadow, only some things. Therefore not all God's attributes, only some of them, show up in His shadow, which is us."

God's attributes are infinite. The same attributes can be found in man but they are finite.

The prayer of the dervish is the prayer of realization. He is ashamed to ask even of God. In the *Fihi Ma Fihi* (*In It Is What Is in It*), Rumi relates that Adam sinned and was expelled from Paradise. "O Adam, when I took you to task and punished you for your sin, why did you not contend with me? You could have said, 'Everything is from You. You created everything. Whatever You will comes to be in the world; whatever You do not will can never come to be.' Why did you not state this clear defense?" "O Lord, I knew

Turkish miniature by Ulker Erke, depicting the *taj* of a Mevlevi sheikh with calligraphy praising Mevlana.

that but I could not be impolite in Your presence. My love for You would not allow me to take You to task."

Here is a perfect example of *adab* (spiritual courtesy), which the Sufi practices within the tariqa and the world. He is content whatever comes. If there is food, it is right. No food, it is right. No covering, it is right. By this contentment he becomes greater than a king. Sitting under a tree, clothed in a patched cloak, he is wealthier than the richest, those who own all the earth and yet are needy, because he has the kingdom of God. His prayer is zikr and *fikr* (of thought only). His presence can spark a heart of stone. On the palms of his hands are written the ninety-nine beautiful names of God.

Rumi's spiritual couplets, known as the *Mathnawi-i Ma'nawi*, are a living scripture which has enlightened the souls of numberless beings. In its simplicity, Rumi expressed the law of life in a series of teaching stories–a style influenced by the Sufi Faridu'd-Din 'Attar. He has chosen the symbol of the reed, separated from the reed bed, as the state of man wandering the earth in the sandals of Moses.

Hazrat Inayat Khan talks of the reed as Rumi's symbol of Man. "There is a beautiful picture Rumi has made. He tells why the melody of the reed flute makes such an appeal to your heart. First it is cut away from its original stem. Then in its heart the holes have been made; and since the holes have been made in the heart, the heart has been broken, and it begins to cry. And so it is with the spirit of the Messenger, with the spirit of the Teacher, that by bearing and by carrying his cross, his self becomes like a reed, hollow. There is scope for the player to play his melody. When it has become nothing, the player takes it to play the melody. If there was something there, the player could not use it. On one end of the reed flute are the lips of the Prophet, and at the other end is to be heard the voice of God.

"God speaks to everyone. It is not only to the Messengers and Teachers. He speaks to the ears of every heart but it is not every heart which hears it. His voice is louder than the thunder, and His light is clearer than the sun–if one could only see it, if one could only hear it. In order to see it and in order to hear it, man should remove this wall, this barrier, which man has made of self.

"Then he becomes the flute upon which the Divine Player may play the music of Orpheus, which can charm even the hearts of stone."

This is the esoteric meaning of the Prophet Muhammad's receiving of the *Kalam-ullah*, the Word of God. The message given Muhammad, in the form of the Koran, is the message of Peace. That is why the religion is called Islam and not Muhammadism. The Prophet was the instrument through which God expressed Himself to man.

The original words of Rumi are so deep that they penetrate the heart of man, and he has been referred to as "the soul of the poet." The *Mathnawi* is man's journey to the Source, to the Beloved.

The lover visible
and the Beloved invisible–
Who ever saw such a love
in all the world?

The spiritual symbol of the flute did not originate with Rumi, although his life is the perfect example of the longing of the reed to be reunited with its stem. An ancient Chinese legend tells of the first music being played on small pieces of reed. The original musician of China cut holes in a piece of reed the distance of two fingers apart, and the reed flute came into being.

In Hindu symbology, Krishna, the god of love, is pictured playing a flute. Divine love enters into man and fills his entire being. The flute is the human heart, and a heart that is made hollow becomes a flute for the god of love to play. The pain and sorrow the soul experiences through life are the holes made in the reed flute. The heart of man is first a reed. The suffering and pain it goes through make it a flute that can then be used by God to produce His music.

Here lies one secret in the zikr of the Sufis. All desires should be eliminated from the heart with the repetition of the negation, la illaha (there is no god) and replaced with the love of God, illa'llah (but God). When nothing but God is remembered, a man's zikr is pure.

The Whirling Dervishes repeat their zikr as they turn to the wailing sound of the *ney*. They empty their hearts of all but the thought of God and whirl in the ecstatic movement of His breath.

The sound of the ney is made by the breath of *Hu* coming from the ney player, who must leave himself and be with Allah. The ney is empty but is given life by the breath of the ney player. Without breath the human being is dead. In the Sufi tradition music has never been an entertainment or a distraction, but is a meditation that reminds one of a state of being.

Because of the universality of his teaching, Rumi became known as the Sultan of Love. Just before he died, he said: "When you see my funeral procession, my body carried on the shoulders of men, do not think that this is a separation, for it is my union with God. When you see the sun rise at dawn and give off great light during the day only to set at evening, it is not a disappearance, but a rebirth of the sun. The light which comes from it is not affected."

As Mevlana's body was placed into the earth, it was as if a seed of love was planted for all men, a seed that bears its fruit in the hearts of learned men. Mevlana spoke of the heavenly spheres and of the hidden treasures buried in the love of God. He lived a diagram of how to complete the weaving of the magic flying carpet and spoke of its real meaning to men who thought that the earth was flat.

Persian miniature by Bihzad c. 1490, showing dervishes dancing in ecstacy. Two *ney* players and a *bendir* player are on the right; behind him a man weeps and others stand with heads bowed. In the foreground several dervishes have swooned; their turbans falling to the ground.

HÂMÛŞÂN

Silent-House (Graveyard)

Top left: A 19th-century posed photograph taken in the tekke showing Mevlevi musicians, semazens and a Koran reader.
Above: 16th-century Persian miniature by Bihzad of Sufi musicians and dancers.
Left: The graveyard, referred to as the Silent-House, at the Galata Mevlevi tekke in Istanbul.

Whatever causes the heart to turn away
from contemplation and knowledge of God
is a veil.

–Rumi

The sema is peace for the souls of the living;
The one who knows this, possesses peace in
    his heart.
The one who wants to be awakened
Is the one who sleeps in the middle of the
    garden.
But for the one who sleeps in prison,
To be awakened is only a nuisance.

–Rumi

Contemporary Turkish miniature by Ulker Erke, of Mevlana Jalalu'ddin Rumi.

Mevlana Jalalu'ddin Rumi

An angel touched him as he slept. In the dreams of three hundred of the most learned men of the city of Balkh, the Mother of Cities, a holy being lifted the right hand of Baha'u-Din Veled and conferred upon him the spiritual name of Sultan Ulema. The following morning all three hundred men came to him and proclaimed themselves his *mureeds* (disciples).

The fame of Baha'u-Din as a spiritual teacher grew to such a point that he became known as "The Elder Master."

On September 30, 1207, a son was born to him and his wife, who was a member of the royal family of Khwarazm. They named the child Jalalu'ddin (the keeper of the faith), and although he lived during a time that witnessed shattering physical blows to the Islamic countries by the Mongols, whose interference altered both the political and spiritual station of the Muslim states, he was to become one of the greatest messengers of Universal Peace ever to walk the planet.

Baha'u-Din Veled foresaw the tragedy of the great city of Balkh, Afghanistan, and its king. His popularity wrought jealousy in the king, and his talk brought controversy to the kingdom. This controversy led to a public address in the great mosque; he predicted the pillage of the Mongols, the destruction of Balkh, and the exile of the king.

He assembled a large caravan, and with his family, friends, and students, he left Balkh to begin the long journey of sixteen summers before permanently settling in Konya.

Jalalu'ddin showed signs of what he was to become as a man. At the age of six he fasted for long periods and saw visions, which his father explained to him as "gifts from the invisible world."

One day as he walked a terraced roof reciting the Koran, he was joined by some other children who proposed that they should all attempt to jump to a neighboring terrace. Jalal said, "These acts of jumping from terrace to terrace are for cats to perform. It is degrading for man whose station is superior. If you are bored, then let us spring up to visit the region of God's realm." As he spoke, he vanished from the sight of the other children. Frightened by the disappearance of their friend, the children began to cry for help. As they cried, Jalal reappeared but with a warm glow on his face and a light in his eyes. He explained that, as he was speaking to them, visible forms dressed in green cloaks had led him away–through the mountains of colors that unfolded great space–to view the concentric orbs of the spheres and the dwelling place of holy beings and the wonders of the world of spirits.

The journey from Balkh was an unchosen journey for some and an unfinished one for others. They traveled over craggy hills, forded rivers, ate the dust scattered by horses' hoofs, and camped on the plains between cities. In the peopled areas they were greeted by holy men, and along the roads dervishes in patched robes bowed to them. Young Jalal sometimes sat in the corner of a covered wagon, eating oranges and figs and listening to his father's mystical teaching stories and Koran readings.

The members of the caravan stopped five times each day to pray. They began each day with the *Salat al-Fajr* that had to be said after dawn but before sunrise. After noon they said the *Salat az-Zuhr* and in the late afternoon the *Salat al-Asr*. The *Salat al-Maghrib* was performed just after sunset, the *Salat al-Isha* at night. So the cycle of their day was interwoven with prayer. At times, the lack of water caused them to perform the holy ablutions with sand. They believed that until the *salik* (traveler) has arrived at the "gate of union," he must continue to work and pray with all his strength. Baha'u-Din's intention was to make the holy pilgrimage to Makkah.

Muhammad b. 'Ali b. Muhammad Ibn al-'Arabi al-Ta'i al-Hatimi, known as Ibn 'Arabi, was one of the greatest of all Sufi masters. During the years of Baha'u-Din's travels, Ibn 'Arabi was making a hajj (pilgrimage) to the Ka'ba in holy Makkah from his home in Seville, Spain.

Of the Ka'ba, al-Ghazzali says, "The Ka'ba [cube] is an outward symbol in the material world of the Presence not seen by the eye, that dwells within the Divine world, just as the body is an outward symbol of this visible phenomenal world, of the heart, which cannot be seen by the eye, for it belongs to the world of the Unseen, and this material, visible world is a means of ascent to the invisible, spiritual world for him to whom God has opened the door."

The pilgrim creates a circular energy around the stationary cube by circumambulating it seven times to represent the seven spheres. He does this three times at a quick pace and four times walking.

During one of the *tawafs*, circumambulations of the Ka'ba, Ibn 'Arabi envisioned a scene that was to mark an important station of his spiritual development. In his *Futuhat*, 'Arabi describes passing a corner of the Ka'ba and meeting a "youth steadfast in devotion," and, by communicating with him, attained a higher awareness of his own true self.

"On one occasion I was circumambulating His ancient House, and while I was engaged in this, praising and glorifying God...I came to the Black Stone and met the eagle stone of the youth steadfast in devotion who is both speaker and silent, neither alive nor dead, both complex and simple, encompassing and encompassed. When I saw him circumambulating the House, the living circumambulating the dead, I grasped what he was and his significance and realized that the circumambulation of the House is like the prayer over the dead.... Then God showed me the spiritual degree of that youth; that he was far beyond all considerations of space and time. When I had realized this...I kissed his right hand...and said to him, 'O bearer of tidings, look and see how I seek your company and desire your friendship.' Then he indicated to me by hint and sign that he was created to speak only by signs.... I begged him to reveal his secrets to me. He said, 'Behold the details of my structure and the order of my formation and you will find the answer to your question set forth in me, for I am not one who speaks or is spoken to, my knowledge being only of myself and my essence being naught other than my names. I am knowledge, the known and the knower.'"

Semazen turning in the garden of Rumi.

'Arabi left Makkah and stopped for twelve days in Baghdad, where, a half century before, Abdul Qadir Gilani lay on his deathbed. Gilani left the sheikh's cloak for a man he said would be coming from the west and would be called Muhyi-d-din. He was the *gauth*, the *qtub* of his time, and made this statement fifty years before 'Arabi came to Baghdad and also before his birth. The qtub (pole of his time) is an appointed being, entirely spiritual of nature, who acts as a divine agent of a sphere at a certain period in time. Each qtub has under him four *awtads* (supports) and a number of *abdals* (substitutes), who aid him in his work of preserving and maintaining the world. Abdul Qadir Gilani was such a being. Before leaving Baghdad, Ibn 'Arabi was given the sheikh's cloak.

In Egypt, the people did not understand 'Arabi and plotted against his life. Unsuccessful attempts were made, which finally caused him to decide to return to Makkah where he stayed a year. From Makkah he traveled north to Asia Minor and remained briefly in Aleppo before arriving in Konya in 1210, the same year the caravan carrying Jalalu'ddin Rumi to Konya left Balkh.

'Arabi stayed in Konya and married the widow of a friend. She had a son whom he adopted. 'Arabi personally trained his stepson in the Sufi doctrine, and the boy, named Sadr al-Din al-Qunawi, became one of the leading spiritual teachers of Konya. Kay Kaus, the ruler of Konya, desired the renowned Andalusian master to remain in his city and presented him with a large house. One day a beggar came to 'Arabi and asked for some money. 'Arabi said: "I have no money; take this house," and then he left Konya.

Baha'u-Din Veled arrived in Baghdad where he was the guest of the eminent Sheikh Shahabu-d-Din Umer Suhreverdi. Before leaving Baghdad, news arrived of the slaughter of Balkh by the forces of Gengis Khan. Fourteen thousand copies of the Koran were burned; fifteen thousand students and professors were slain; two hundred thousand adult males were fatally pierced by the arrows of the Grand Khan's army. The intelligence and future of Balkh was erased. The birthplace of Jalalu'ddin Rumi was razed.

The journey continued as the travelers came to Makkah and performed the great pilgrimage. Makkah and Madinah offered them the holy vibrations of their beloved Muhammad and gave them the strength to continue their nomadic lifestyle.

In Nishapur, Iran, they met with the Sufi Faridu'd-Din 'Attar who gave young Jalal his blessings and a copy of his *Book of Mysteries.* He told Baha'u-Din, "The day will come when this child will kindle the fire of divine enthusiasm throughout the world."

'Attar was a chemist. One day a wandering dervish came to his dispensary for alms but received no reply from the busy proprietor. A second time the dervish asked and was ignored. "You are so busy becoming wealthy here, how will you depart from this world forced to leave all you have amassed?" 'Attar replied, "Like you, I will give up my ghost." The dervish lay down, closed his eyes, and, repeating the name of God, passed on. For 'Attar this was an initiation. He closed his shop, distributed his wealth to the poor, and became a dervish and a scholar. The most famous of his 114 books are the *Memoirs of the Saints* and *The Conference of the Birds.*

Baha'u-Din Veled and the Sufi 'Attar sat together, drank the customary tea, and spoke of passages in the Koran. Several hours later the travelers were preparing to depart. As young Jalal walked closely behind his father, 'Attar turned to one of the dervishes and remarked, "Look at this peculiar situation; there goes a sea followed by an ocean." (The essence of this story is true, although some scholars attribute the incident as having occurred in the presence of Ibn 'Arabi.)

The caravan passed through Damascus, where it is said Baha'u-Din Veled and Ibn 'Arabi once met, and then remained for four years near Arzanjan in Armenia (Erzincan in present-day Turkey). Ismet Khatun, wife of the local ruler, built Baha'u-Din a college where he stayed and taught until both she and her husband died. The caravan then traveled to Karaman (Laranda) where Jalalu'ddin married a young woman named Gevher Khatun–the daughter of Sherefeddin Lala, one of the followers from Balkh.

On this peregrination, many towns asked Rumi's father to remain. "If you build a *medrese*, a school for me, I will stay." Karaman, a center of learning sixty miles south of Konya, built him a school, and he stayed. It was here that Rumi's mother died. Baha'u-Din's fame as a great theologian and mystic spread throughout the land.

By now Jalalu'ddin had become a scholar well-versed in the Koran and in some of the secrets of the life of dervishes. He began to understand the power of keeping a secret so that the implanted seed might have time to go through its inner process of growth and bear flowers and fruits. He knew that which is kept within and nourished would be preserved and that which one gives out is dispersed. Although the mouth speaks the name of God, closed lips retain that name.

Sultan Alaeddin Keykubat sent for Baha'u-Din and offered him a great university if he would come and share his learning with the people of Konya.

Konya, known as the holy city, is one of the oldest continuously inhabited towns and, according to Phrygian legend, was the first place to emerge after the Flood. At various times in history Konya had been inhabited by the Hittites, Phrygians, Persians, Pergamese, and the Romans. During the time of the Romans its name was changed from Iconium to Claudiconium in honor of the Emperor Claudius. In the first century, St. Paul and St. Barnabas preached there. From the seventh to the thirteenth century, the city suffered various Arab raids and occupations. The Seljuks captured it, lost it to the Crusaders, and recaptured it. Control was finally lost to the Emirate of Karaman until Sultan Mehmet the Conqueror declared Konya an Ottoman city in 1476. It remained under Ottoman rule until 1923 when Mustapha Kemal led a military revolution and made all of Turkey a Republic. Kemal gave himself the name Ataturk (father of Turkey) and was Turkey's leader until his death in 1938.

Two Mevlevis turning in contemplation.

The essence of the heart of man is eternal and does not change. Culture, religion, beliefs, and history all change with time. Konya as a city is a thousand years old and has changed its name, its size, its architecture, and its inhabitants many times. From a Byzantium city to an Islamic one, from an Ottoman city to a part of a Republic, the city changes but the state of its humanity continues to live. All who have resided there tell their story in their own language. The language of Rumi is for everyone in every age. The deep feeling of Mevlana opens the heart, bridges the dialogue of culture, and through Mevlana man sees the human treasures. Rumi lived his life in Konya. It was his horizon, his laboratory, and he proved that the desire of the heart of man has no boundaries.

In 1226 when Baha'u-Din Veled came to the Seljuk capital of Konya with his family and friends, the city was experiencing a cultural regeneration under the leadership of Sultan Alaeddin.

One day Sultan Alaeddin invited Baha'u-Din to climb his terraced roof and observe the walls and towers he had erected to fortify Konya.

Baha'u-Din remarked, "Against torrents and the horsemen of the enemy you have put a good defense. What protection do you have from the sighs and moans of the oppressed that leap a thousand walls? Go and attempt to acquire the blessings of your subjects. This is the real stronghold."

Baha'u-Din was the revered university professor and advisor to the Sultan until his death in 1228. The lectures he gave at the university were collected by his students in three volumes and eventually published under the title of *Maarif*. His son, Jalalu'ddin Rumi, a noble scholar of theology, became his successor and attracted hundreds of students from all areas of the Anatolian plateau who accepted him as his father's sole spiritual heir.

There are many unknown teachers in the world sharing in a variety of duties regarding its maintenance. Sheikh Hajjaj, one of the close disciples of Baha'u-Din Veled, was such a being. After the death of his teacher, Sheikh Hajjaj left the college and returned to his trade as a weaver. The meal he prepared to break his daily fast was coarse brown bread made of unsifted flour which he would mash with water. He saved his earnings, carried them to the college, and placed them in the shoes of his teacher's son, Jalalu'ddin Rumi. When Sheikh Hajjaj died, a professional washer was appointed to perform the final ablution on the body. As he washed the body and was about to touch the private parts of the deceased, the dead man grasped his hand with an iron grip, causing him to cry from pain and fright. No one was able to loosen the grip. Jalalu'ddin arrived, and he whispered into the ear of the dead Sheikh Hajjaj, "This poor man is unaware of your high station. Forgive his unintentional transgression for my sake." Immediately the poor washer's hand was released, but three days later he, too, was being washed in preparation for his grave.

Calligraphy repeating the name of the Prophet Muhammad (may the peace and blessings of Allah be upon him).

One who has the title of Seyyid is a direct descendant of the Prophet Muhammad. In 1230, Seyyid Burhan al-Din Muhaqqiq, a close friend and mureed of Rumi's father in Balkh, arrived in Konya. He was a true dervish who had lived in the solitude of the mountains in a state of mystical ecstasy.

Upon his arrival in Konya, Seyyid was informed that his friend and teacher had been dead a year. He decided to stay and devote his life to the spiritual training of Jalalu'ddin Rumi. For the next nine years Rumi was initiated into a knowledge possessed by the prophets and saints entitled "The Science of Divine Intuition." During these years he traveled to Aleppo and Damascus with his teacher.

At the end of the ninth year, when he was certain that the knowledge he had received from his teacher had now been passed on to Jalalu'ddin, Seyyid said, "Your training is now complete. Go and flood the souls of men with new life and immeasurable grace. Revive the dead of this world of appearance with the message and your love." He then journeyed to Kayseri and prepared for his death. He instructed his servant to bring an ewer of warm water and then to leave him. As the servant left the room the Seyyid said, "Go and proclaim that the Seyyid has departed to the other world." Then he bolted the door.

Inside the room, the Seyyid performed ablutions, arranged his clothing, lay down on the couch and said, "All of the angels, saints, those known and unknown, who have entrusted a secret to me, come now and receive back your charges." He died with the name of God on his lips and in his heart.

Hearing of the death of his spiritual teacher, Rumi went to Kayseri, collected his teacher's books and papers, said the Fatihah at the Seyyid's tomb, and returned to Konya to resume his position at the university.

Jalalu'ddin slept little. He passed his days and nights in worship of God and became an ocean of knowledge in all temporal and spiritual subjects. He was reaching the station of "walking on water." The universe is an ocean of vibrations and each movement is a wave. The great devotees pray to be liberated that they may be able to swim in this ocean, and the greatest of devotees are able to rise above the waves of this vast ocean of life where so many are drowned. To be in the world but not of it is to walk on water, to be unaffected by the world. The constant repetition of zikr was carrying Rumi above the concepts of the earth.

Rumi had the ability to trace a man's past and read his future by experiencing his presence. The power of zikr developed the healing power of his voice so that the vibrations and breath that accompanied his words had a healing effect on those being addressed.

Often during a zikr circle, a deputy sheikh would walk in the inner part of the circle carrying an open bottle of water and would place the water before each dervish's mouth as he said "Allah." Later, this water, made holy by the breath vibration of the name of God, would be given to a sick person in the community to drink. At times the clothing of the sick person would be placed in the center of the circle to gain the "energy beams" of the zikr. By contemplating God's presence, Rumi's heart gained great warmth and made his presence a power that erased the ills of the mind and its adverse effects on the body. The written word of a man like Rumi became a charm, and when he played an instrument the vibrations that came forth into the air could heal.

One day, as he sat in his garden, Rumi was called to the house of one of his disciples who was suffering from an intermittent fever. He took a pen and paper and wrote, "If you believe in God, the Most Great, make not the head to ache; vitiate not the swallow; eat not the flesh; drink not the blood; and depart from this being. I bear witness that there is no god save God, and I testify that Muhammad is His servant and apostle." Then he washed the ink from the paper and gave the solution to the patient to drink. The man was immediately relieved of his illness.

In the next years, Rumi continued to teach at the university, to conduct zikr circles, and to spend time in the training of his two sons. He would often attend the lectures of his friend, Sadr al-Din al-Qunawi, the stepson of Ibn 'Arabi. Qunawi spoke on the teachings of 'Arabi which, although their roots were in religion, broke these barriers and taught of love on the universal level.

As Rumi entered the room to hear his friend speak, Qunawi said, "Come and sit with me on the post" (the sheepskin on which the sheikh sits). Rumi looked at him and remarked, "Two cannot sit on one skin." Qunawi got up, took the skin from under him, and flung it away saying, "I don't need this anymore."

This act of eliminating the separation represented the passing of the 'Arabi teachings to Rumi, linking the 'Arabi and Mevlevi line, the path of knowledge and the path of love.

In 1244, Shamsi Tabriz arrived in Konya. He wore an old, patched, black wool cloak and had no possessions. Shams, the sun, was known as *parinda* (winged one) because he had wandered in many lands seeking spiritual teachers. Shams' journey began when he left the city of Tabriz in Persia in search of the highest levels of absolute perfection. He had been prepared for this stage of his development by the unique and holy spiritual teacher of Tabriz, Sheikh Abu Bakr, who was known as the Thresher. When Sheikh Abu Bakr asked what he would give to see the Truth, Shams answered, "My head."

During his travels in search of "one of His beings loved and veiled" (a qtub), Shams would stop at *khanaqas* (Sufi monasteries), visit with the hermit dervishes residing in the mountains, do zikr with sheikhs in clay-walled rooms of dust-ridden villages, and seek out the teachers of the cities in the hope of seeing the beloved face of the Hidden Master. His love of God was so great, the radiance of his being so glowing, his overwhelming power so unapproachable and unpredictable that few could stand beside him. By his tests of their love of God he turned spiritual teachers into his servants and disciples. In Baghdad he encountered Sheikh Aluhad-ed-din of Kirman.

"What are you doing?" asked Shams.

"I am looking at the moon in this lake."

"Unless you suffer from a boil on your neck, why not look at the sky? Are you so blind that you do not see the true object in all you contemplate?"

The sheikh replied that he wished to become Shams' disciple and to travel with him.

"You do not have the strength to bear my company," replied Shams.

"The strength is within me," said the sheikh. "Please accept me."

"Then bring me a pitcher of wine, and we will drink together in the Baghdad market."

Thinking of public opinion and what he was taught, the sheikh replied, "I cannot do this."

Shams shouted, "You are too timid for us! It is the wine of love that makes one God-intoxicated. You haven't the strength to be among the intimate friends of God. I seek only Him who knows how to reach Truth."

In the East, wise men were called *balakesh*, meaning "He who took the draught of all difficulties." The difficulties of life were regarded as a wine that, once drunk, would disappear. The Sufi is one who accepts all things.

One cold November morning, the wanderings of this mysterious being who walked in a field of magnetism brought him to the front of the Shekerjiler Hani (Inn of the Sugar Merchants) in Konya just as Mevlana (Our Master) Jalalu'ddin Rumi was passing. Mevlana Jalalu'ddin sat majestically on his horse as his students scrambled to walk beside him and hold

Shams opened the heart of Rumi, and Rumi became an eloquent tongue for Shams, revealing his inner teachings and love for the Prophet Muhammad.

the stirrup. He had just completed his class at the College of Cotton Merchants and with a throng of students was passing the Inn of the Sugar Merchants. Shams leapt from the crowd, grasped the bridle of the horse, and shouted: "O teacher of the Muslims, who was greater, Abu Yazid Bistami or Muhammad the Prophet?" Rumi felt the eyes of Shams look past his own into the very essence of his being, causing rivers of energy to flow within his body. "The Prophet Muhammad was greater," replied Rumi. Then Shams said, "Did not the Prophet say, 'We have not known Thee as Thou deserves to be known,' while Abu Yazid exclaimed, 'How great is my glory; I am exalted; my dignity is upraised; I am the sultan of sultans?'" Mevlana answered, "Abu Yazid's thirst was quenched after a mouthful, but the Prophet of God sought for water, thirsting more and more. Abu Yazid satisfied himself with what he attained in God, but Muhammad the 'Elect One of God' sought each day further, and from hour to hour and day to day saw light and power and divine wisdom increase. That is why he said, 'We have not known Thee as Thou shouldest be known.'"

Mihrab, **indicating the direction of prayer, in the Mevlevi semahane, Konya, Turkey.**

Shams cried to God and fell to the ground. Mevlana dismounted, dropped to his knees, touched the head of Shams, and the two men embraced.

They left the questioning students and retired to a retreat cell where they remained for three months, occupied with the exploration of awakening. The two men merged as one being in the fatherhood of God. They became their own planet. Mevlana was the earth; his function was to uplift the consciousness of man, revolving around and finally merging with Shams, the sun. They were stirred to the depths of their beings and transfigured by the joy of life. Lost in God-consciousness, they experienced the ecstasy of which the Sufis speak. Here within the stone walls of a small domed *chille* (retreat) hut was a friendship based on the discovery of God through each other at a time when both beings had a lesson to impart to one another.

Shams was a catalyst to the sheikhs. Sultan Veled, Rumi's son, once remarked of Shams that "His glory was veiled even from those who were themselves veiled in the glory of God." The spirit of the meeting of Jalalu'ddin and Shams was imbued with Divine Light. These beings, face to face, saw within each other the grace and presence of the essence of what each sought. For the first time each could reveal to another being the secret in his heart. Rumi was like a room filled with God-love. Shams saw this and opened the door. As they meditated on the Beloved, sounded *wasifas* (attributes of God) and the zikr (la illaha illa'llah, there is no god but God), the air in the small hut was made pure by the breath of these two holy beings.

Rumi later wrote in the *Diwan-i Shamsi Tabriz:*

> Happy the moment when we are seated in the palace, thou and I,
> With two forms and with two figures but with one soul, thou and I.

The colors of the grove and the voice of the birds will bestow
>   immortality
At the time when we come into the garden, thou and I.
The stars of heaven will come to gaze upon us;
We shall show them the moon itself, thou and I.
Thou and I, individuals no more, shall be mingled in ecstasy,
Joyful and secure from foolish babble, thou and I.
All the bright-plumed birds of heaven will devour their hearts
>   with envy
In the place where we shall laugh in such a fashion, thou and I.
This is the greatest wonder, that thou and I, sitting here in the
>   same nook,
Are at this moment both in Iraq and Khorasan, thou and I.

Outside the stone hut Rumi's students missed the discourses and direction of their beloved teacher. Their thoughts turned to jealousy, and they began to question the identity of the poorly clad, black-bearded dervish, whom Rumi would later refer to as "a king in a patched robe." How could it be that such a great man, himself the son of a great saint, could be seduced by this stranger to Konya?

As his mureeds sank into the sea of confusion, grasping at weightless rumors, Mevlana Jalalu'ddin sat before Shamsi Tabriz and saw his own soul in the mirror of Shams' heart. The thin veil of the zikr which often hides the Beloved was finally lifted, and they knew the words of Mansur al-Hallaj, who said, "It is Thou that castest me into ecstasy, not the zikr," and the words of the greatest woman Sufi saint, Rabia al-Adawiya, "Love of God hath so absorbed me that neither love nor hate of any other thing remains in my heart."

At times Shams would bow to the feet of Mevlana and kiss his hand, and at other times he would confront the spiritual master of Konya with the most trying tasks.

Caught in the jealousy of losing the interest of their beloved teacher, the students of Mevlana could not lift the veil of ignorance to ask themselves what it was that these two God-intoxicated men did for one hundred and one consecutive days which caused them to have cosmic effulgence, to emanate such peace from the depths of their beings, to leave their worldly attachments. They did not ask themselves how man can reach this state so necessary for his inner growth and yet so distant from his earthly reach. The presence of Shamsi Tabriz produced rare light in the being of Mevlana and suffocated the ambitions of his students and close friends. The sun shone and also darkened the hearts of many of those around Mevlana who were satisfied simply to know a secret rather than to practice it.

Mevlana once said, "When Shams comes to me and speaks, the fire of

---

The true sultan, said Rumi, is Shams, the king in a patched robe.

54

mystic love shoots a flame into my heart." Shams instructed Mevlana to study the teachings of his father, to keep silent and to speak to no one. Jalalu'ddin's love for this being was so great that he unquestioningly followed the guidance. This caused further unrest among his students. During this time Shams came to Jalalu'ddin while he was studying his father's writings and told him to close the books. This Jalalu'ddin did and never opened them again.

One night Jalalu'ddin dreamed that he and some friends were studying and discussing the teachings of his father. As he woke from the dream, Shams entered his room and said, "I told you not to study this book." Jalalu'ddin said that he had not once opened the book since Shams' instruction. Shams said, "There is study by reading and there is study by contemplating. Dreams are the shadows of our waking thoughts. If you did not occupy your thoughts with these works, you would not have dreamt about them." It was at times like these that Shams showed the greatness bestowed upon a man who holds God as his Beloved.

Some said that Shams was illiterate and had no formal schooling, but one day Mevlana told his mureeds that Shams was a great alchemist and scholar in all the sciences, but that he renounced them all to devote himself to the study and contemplation of the mysteries of divine love.

In the *Fihi Ma Fihi*, Rumi discusses the "illiteracy" of the Prophet Muhammad.

"The Prophet is not called 'unlettered' because he was unable to write. He was called that because his 'letters,' his knowledge and wisdom were innate, not acquired. What can partial intellect have that universal intellect has not? The partial intellect is not capable of inventing anything it has not seen before. Recall the story of the raven: when Cain killed Abel and stood not knowing what to do with the body. One raven killed another, dug out the earth, buried the dead raven and scratched the earth over the body. From this Cain learned how to dig a grave and bury a body. All trades are like this. The possessor of partial intellect requires instruction while those who have united the partial with the universal intellect and become one are prophets and saints."

Although most of Mevlana's students had animus toward Shams, there were some, like Husamuddin, who showed him great respect and service. Shams told Husam that religion was a question of money. "Give me your money and offer your services to the Lord." Husam went home, collected all his valuables, his wife's jewels, money, and provisions and laid them at Shams' feet. He sold his property in the village of Filaras and brought the money to Shams, thanking him for having taught him a duty and for accepting such an insignificant amount from his hand.

Shams looked at him with great love and said: "It is hoped that with the prayers of the saints and God's grace, you will attain such a station as to be the envy of the most perfect men of God and bowed down to by the Brotherhood of Sincerity. It is true that men of God are not in want of anything, being independent of both worlds, but the sure way to test the sincerity of the ones we love and the affection of a friend is to ask him to sacrifice his worldly possessions. The second request is to ask him to give up all that is not his God. No disciple who wishes to rise has ever made progress by following his own devices. Advancement is earned by rendering service and by spending in God's cause. Enlightenment is not a fixed place. It is as much at the bottom of the mountain as it is on the top. It is in the beginning of every movement as well as the end."

Shams then returned to Husam ten times the amount of goods he gave. Years later, Jalalu'ddin made Husam the keeper of God's treasury and chose him to write down the spiritual couplets which he recited. These couplets became the *Mathnawi* that the Sufi poet Abdur Rahman Jami called "the Koran in Persian..." and that led him to say of Rumi, "Though he is not a prophet, he has a Book."

Shams was a *madhoub* (one lost in contemplation of God), and, like all those with the task of awakening man from his semi-slumber, his actions were unpredictable. Once when Mevlana was giving a discourse to some close mureeds, Shams took his books and threw them into a pool of water, saying, "You must live what you know." When a disturbed Rumi moved to save his books, Shams told him that the theoretical knowledge in his books was meaningless, but if they meant so much to him he could remove them from the pool, and they would be dry.

Another day, Shams addressed Rumi's mureeds and said, "I will tell you a secret so that Mevlana Jalalu'ddin shall not hear. A single farthing of his is worth a hundred thousand dinars to me. Whoever comes to me is submitted to him, for a door was shut and he has opened it. To know Mevlana, I am imperfect; I know him imperfectly, for each day I observe in him some state, action, or quality that was not there before. Understand Mevlana a little better if you wish to gain peace. He is the very form of truth. He pronounces fine words; don't be satisfied with them, for behind each is something you should ask him."

As the dervish brothers walked the dirt streets of Konya, they repeated the name of God with each step and the entire atmosphere became an inspiration that evoked wonderful thoughts. During one of these walks Shams turned to Jalalu'ddin and said, "When I was a child, I saw God; I saw angels; I watched the mysteries of the higher and lower worlds. I thought all men saw the same. At last I realized that they did not see. Then my sheikh, Sheikh Abu Bakr, forbade me to speak of these things."

Explaining these words to his mureeds, Mevlana said, "This was Shams himself. It came to him from eternity, not from his austerities and devotion."

Mevlana wrote in the *Diwan-i Shamsi Tabriz*:

The man of God is drunken without wine,
The man of God is full without meat.
The man of God is distraught and bewildered,
The man of God has no food or sleep.
The man of God is a king beneath a dervish-cloak,
The man of God is a treasure in a ruin.
The man of God is not of air and earth,
The man of God is not of fire and water.
The man of God is a boundless sea,
The man of God rains pearls without a cloud.
The man of God hath hundred moons and skies,
The man of God hath hundred suns.
The man of God is made wise by the Truth,
The man of God is not learned from books.
The man of God is beyond infidelity and religion,
To the man of God right and wrong are alike,
The man of God has ridden away from Not-being,
The man of God is gloriously attended.
The man of God is concealed, Shams-ed-Din;
The man of God do thou seek and find!

Part of a wall with calligraphy depicting the word *Hu* (Him), in the Mevlevi Museum which Kemal Attaturk allowed to be opened in 1927 on the site of the Mevlevi tekke in Konya.

The man of God drunk without wine is the perfect Sufi. The great Sufi poet Hafiz also spoke of the dervish as a king in a patched robe. "Despise not thou the poor who Love obey; unbelted monarchs, crownless kings are they."

Sufi poets often refer to the hidden treasure that Rumi hints of in the last line of this poem. Jami asserts on the authority of the *Kashfu'l Mahjub* that there are four thousand saints "unacquainted with each other and ignorant of their exalted state who are always hidden from themselves and others."

In the Orient there is a belief that there are forty beings who take care of the world and are unknown to each other and who, at times, are even unknown to themselves. Therefore they greet each person with a bow and a smile for they are unaware of the station of the being they are addressing.

One beautiful moonlit night, Jalalu'ddin and Shams were on the terraced roof of the college while the inhabitants of Konya were sleeping on their housetops. Shams remarked, "Look at all these poor creatures. They are dead to every sense of their Creator on this beautiful night." Turning to Jalalu'ddin, he said, "Won't you, from your infinite compassion, wake them up and let them share in the blessings of this night?"

Each day of their relationship, Shams subtly showed Jalalu'ddin that his spiritual powers had to be used on a universal level. Shams often caused friction in the lives of the sheikhs and teachers of Konya. This friction brewed anger in them rather than enlightenment in having the opportunity to view their real selves. At a gathering of sheikhs, Shams once remarked, "If you have some business to do, then why do you do nothing? If you have none, then where is your concern? You play the cymbals, and no noise is heard; you work, but no one profits.

"If you follow the path of religion, for a long time you reach neither village nor inn. You see no signs. No bark of dog or crowing of cock reaches your ears. It is a strange path. You march so long, yet seem to stay in the same place."

There is a tale of a wandering Sufi who, by chance, came upon a small grove of oak trees, whose branches interlocked to form a natural shelter against the sun and rain. It was an insignificant grove, one of many, and the few passersby did not notice its existence. The Sufi stayed the night and decided to live and meditate in the grove.

He lived there for many years, sheltered from both the sun and rain. He left the grove once a week to gather food but returned within a few hours to continue his prayers for enlightenment. For all his persistence, his prayers remained unanswered. At times, the Sufi suspected that the interlocking branches, which kept the elements out, were holding his prayers in so that they reached no further than the underside of the topmost level.

He remained hopeful, and the grove itself, as if to strengthen his hope, flourished. The branches of the oak trees were covered with an abundance of green foliage. The beauty of the grove was the only encouragement given to the Sufi, although he meditated for many years. Finally he grew despondent. His efforts seemed fruitless, his goal as distant as ever.

So it was that eighteen years after his arrival, the Sufi left the grove one dark night and never returned. All through that night the abandoned grove continued to glow mysteriously, as though it still sheltered an aspiring holy man.

By chance, early the next morning, a beggar passed by the grove. He was a simple man, neither particularly good nor evil, one caught up in his trouble. Yet so magnetic was the grove that the beggar felt himself impelled toward it and then pulled into its recesses.

Once inside, he became a different person. As though responding to a spoken command, this humble man took the Sufi's former place. Now, he, too, began to pray. Throughout the rest of that day and night, the grove's new occupant meditated. He repeated strange words that he didn't know he knew. Curious sounds stirred within his body, rising from his chest to his throat, and although the sound emerged from his mouth, the vibrations seemed to go up and out through the top of his head. He felt above all things, and just before the first light of day he became enlightened.

Of all the sheikhs, only Jalalu'ddin could "bear the presence" of Shams, this unknown sheikh of sheikhs who had come to disrupt their lives, to break them down, wash away their smugness, and have them rebuild themselves with a trace of the traceless.

The anger of those who loved Mevlana grew. One Thursday in 1246, after a stay of sixteen months, Shams left Konya and journeyed to Damascus. After a long absence he returned to Konya at the request of Mevlana. Again the two dervish brothers went into a retreat cell where they sat knee to knee, fasting and performing constant zikr, and again the students and friends of Mevlana, who had enjoyed his presence daily during the absence of Shams, became jealous. They plotted to drive away this magician who stole their time with their beloved Mevlana.

Once again the burning jealousy and dudgeon of Mevlana's students drove Shams into exile. He returned to Damascus, where at times he was forced to take menial jobs, doing difficult physical work in order to balance that part of him which was so overwhelmed with God-consciousness. Shams was a man who walked on the earth and, at the same time, lived in another world. He lived within the depths of his heart, within the depths of his soul, and had the power of great intuition, visions, and revelations.

Calligraphy praising Mevlana is in the shape of a Mevlevi sheikh's *destar*. Hattat Hamid al-Amidi of Istanbul designed this in 1381 H.

In Konya, Mevlana longed for his beloved soul brother. He became distraught and spent long hours alone in the room he had shared with Shams. He wept, sometimes from joy, sometimes from loneliness.

Finally, he called for his son, Sultan Veled, and told him to go to Damascus, locate Shams, and beg him to return to Konya. Sultan Veled found Shams on Salihiyye Mountain playing backgammon with a young French boy. The twenty friends who accompanied Sultan Veled remained at the door to the inn until the game was concluded. As they entered the room of the game, the French boy was arguing with Shams over the winnings. The visitors all bowed to Shams with great respect and each approached him and kissed his hand. Pangs of fear fluttered through the boy's body as he realized the stature of his friend. With the palm of his right hand, Shams touched the boy's head and instructed him to return to France and visit certain dervishes residing there. While in the company of this unknown holy man, the young French boy was given *baraka* (divine grace). A seed was planted which would bear fruit for a future civilization. Years later, on the continent, he became known as a great teacher of esoteric knowledge.

Shams embraced Sultan Veled and asked after the health of his father. As Shams spoke with Sultan Veled, two thousand pieces of gold were strewn at his feet by the trusted friends who made the journey to Damascus. Shams, also longing for the company of Mevlana, agreed to return to Konya.

Sultan Veled walked at the stirrup of Shams' horse from Damascus to Konya. When they arrived at the inn of Zindjirli, just outside the city, a dervish was sent ahead to announce their arrival. A great crowd awaited them and witnessed the long embrace of Mevlana and Shams.

Shams blessed Sultan Veled and prayed that, with the permission of God, he might become a great sheikh.

Later, Sultan Veled wrote of Shams, "Shams began to speak and pearls came from his mouth. He sowed a new love in my heart and soul. He revealed secrets to me about the Koran and the Prophet Muhammad. He taught me to fly without wings. He unveiled my eyes so that I could see night as dawn. He took me to the boundless sea where I found inner peace. I experienced a feeling of freedom, like a bird no longer caged, and a safety and protection from every manner of danger." These feelings are evident in the sema today, which was choreographed by Sultan Veled.

The separation of Mevlana and Shams brought them even closer than before to the God in each of them. The hadith states, "Allah, who cannot fit into the entire universe, can fit into the heart of a believer."

They kindled the light within themselves and set their hearts aflame in Godness until Mevlana cried with joy, "Enough of phrases and conceits and metaphors, I want burning, burning, burning."

Mevlana's students were so caught up in their personal love for him that they failed to see the manner of his life. They plotted to slay Shams.

On a Tuesday night in May 1247, Shamsi Tabriz left the side of his beloved spiritual brother and stepped into the garden. His killers circled him and stabbed at his flesh. From the depths of his soul came the cry, *"La illa-ha illa Ana"* (There is no God but Me), and it was these words, uttered with Shams' last breath, that shattered the consciousness of his slayers. When they awoke, all they found were a few drops of blood. The body of Shams had disappeared and no trace of it has ever been found.

> As the sun moving, clouds behind him run,
> All hearts attend thee, O Tabriz's Sun!

Those close to Mevlana busied themselves with a month-long search for Shams, while the despondent soul mate, as if ripped of flesh like Abraham's proverbial sheep, cried from the pain and longing of his separation from the Beloved.

Mevlana refused to believe that Shams was dead and asked every traveler who came to Konya if they had seen his beloved brother. One day a traveler told him that he had seen Shams in Damascus. Mevlana was so pleased that he removed his robe and gave it to the stranger. When it was pointed out to him that the story was probably fabricated for his benefit, Mevlana said, "I have given my turban and gown for a lie. I would have given my life for the truth."

He who was known as *hadi* (the guide), *khabir* (he who is aware), *wali* (the nearest friend), parinda (the winged one); he who was a catalyst to the sheikhs, a lover of God, unknown to the known and known to the unknown;

he who was known as Shams (the sun) of Tabriz, the beloved of Mevlana Jalalu'ddin Rumi, has left this place.

Mevlana refused to see anyone. He confined himself to his house and would often whirl around one of the architectural poles in his garden. On the fortieth day after the murder, he ordered mourning robes, a white shirt open at the chest, and a honey-colored wool fez. He became the madhoub that Shams was, and, intoxicated with love of God, he made wailing sounds with his heart and yearned for union with the Beloved. He cried out in spiritual verse and uttered phrases and spiritual jewels that later would be known as the beginning of the *Mathnawi*.

Istanbul Mevlevi Sheikh Selman Tuzun turning in the fourth *selam* of a sema in Konya.

> Hearken to this Reed forlorn,
> Breathing, even since 'twas torn
> From its rushy bed, a strain
> Of impassioned love and pain.
> The secret of my song, though near,
> None can see and none can hear.
> Oh, for a friend to know the sign
> And mingle all his soul with mine!
> 'Tis the flame of Love that fired me,
> 'Tis the wine of Love inspired me.
> Wouldst thou learn how lovers bleed,
> Hearken, hearken to the Reed!

He became thin in the earthly sense by fasting yet was full in the ecstasy of losing himself in God-consciousness. He became annihilated and glorified with every step.

As with the Prophet before him, the angels descended to earth, opened his breast, and removed the thin shell that remained over his heart. They removed the last bit of ego that remained within him and filled his heart with Love. Then they made his breast as it was before. As this was happening, Mevlana was in his garden lost in deep meditation, in a state of disassociation from his body, experiencing the highest initiation he would know until his "wedding day."

When he regained earth-consciousness, he felt as if the heart of his beloved Shams was merged with his own. He was now ready to re-enter the world.

Rumi was aware of Allah in all things. Prayer, and the remembrance of Allah, were his primary concerns. He told his mureeds: "If you are mindful of Allah, little by little your interior will be illuminated and you will attain release from the world. If you have musk in a container with a narrow neck, you put your finger into it. You can't get the musk out, but your finger is perfumed nonetheless and your sense of smell is gratified. Being mindful of Allah is like this. Although you cannot reach His essence, remembrance of

Him has many effects, and many great benefits accrue."

After the disappearance of Shams, Sultan Veled wrote: "The Shamseddin we were looking for has returned. While we slept, he changed his clothes and came back. He is among us, for after you drink the Heavenly wine, the wine is the same even if the cup is changed."

Salahu'ddin Zerkub, the goldbeater, was a dervish brother to Jalalu'ddin when they were both students of Seyyid Burhanu'ddin. After the death of Shams they renewed their friendship, and Rumi's son, Sultan Veled, married Fatima, the daughter of Salahu'ddin. Rumi was fond of his daughter-in-law and taught her the Koran. He referred to Fatima as his right eye, to her younger sister Hediyya as his left eye, and called their mother, Latifa Khatun, the personification of God's grace.

Salahu'ddin, the goldbeater, remained Rumi's close disciple until his death in December 1258. During those years Mevlana recited the first books of the *Mathnawi,* and Salahu'ddin wrote them down. Mevlana wrote the first eighteen lines of the *Mathnawi* and spoke the remainder as discourses given in the Persian language.

Through Shams, Mevlana had become a poet and a lover of music. One day, as he walked by the goldbeater's shop, he heard the hammers of the apprentices pounding the rough sheets of gold into beautiful objects. With each step he repeated the name of God; and now with the sound of the hammers beating the gold, all he heard was "Allah, Allah."

"Allah, Allah" became every sound he heard, and he began to whirl in ecstasy in the middle of the street. He unfolded his arms, like a fledgling bird, clasped his robe, tilted his head back, and whirled, whirled, whirled to the sound of "Allah" that came forth from his heart and the very wind he created by his movement.

> I see the waters which spring from their sources,
> The branches of trees which dance like penitents,
> The leaves which clap their hands like minstrels.

This was the beginning of the Mevlevi Order of Sufis, known in the West as the Whirling Dervishes. With the continuing outpouring of verse coming from Mevlana, the task of copying it down was given to his friend and disciple Husamuddin Hasan.

Husam was praised by Mevlana as "the light of truth, a soul polishing light, the sword (*Husam*) of religion and love, generous Husamuddin."

During the next ten years Husam acted as Mevlana's deputy sheikh, inspiring his writings to such a degree that Mevlana referred to the *Mathnawi* as "the book of Husam."

As the cold winters of Konya turned to spring, Mevlana and his friends would often go to Husam's large house on a hilltop overlooking the city.

Here, in the village of Meram, five miles west of Konya, Mevlana would walk the fruit orchards or sit by the flowering trees and give discourses to his mureeds. Rumi would often whirl in the garden, his arms close to his body, holding his robe. His nature was filled with kindness, and so he allowed his disciples to embrace him gently as he turned, and, for a short time, to turn with him.

A similar movement can be seen in the *Bedevi Topu* of the Halveti dervishes. The sheikh breaks the turning zikr circle and holds the hands, crossed at the wrists, of one of his dervishes. They slowly turn together, repeating the Name of Allah. The other dervishes form concentric circles around them with the blessing of the inner reaching the outermost circle.

Also in Meram was a small mosque and a prayer room where Mevlana would meet with his mureeds and perform a sema (whirling dance). It was here, during these *sohbets,* spiritual discourses, that much of the *Fihi Ma Fihi* was collected.

The mosque is a private place within an area that is public. The dome of the mosque has been compared to a cosmic crypt or cosmic house and the tall thin minaret to man in an ancient prayer stance. It describes man, the only being in the world who stands upright. From a tiny circular porch at the top of the minaret, the *muezzin* chants the Muslim call to prayer five times each day. The minaret (place where light shines) is the lighthouse for those lost in the sea of life. It is a guide to the traveler and marks a holy place. But, more than the minaret, the perfect man is the holy place.

The one known as Old Baba had seen over one hundred Konya winters. He was a friend to Mevlana and a spiritual guide to the people of Meram where he lived. Although he was too old to cook the large meals which Mevlana had served in commune style, Old Baba was given the honor of salting the food at Mevlana's table. After his death in 1268, the Imam of the Meram mosque began the practice of giving a small packet of salt to each visitor to his tomb, a practice still continued today.

Many people visited the tomb of Baba, who lived 130 years. Among them was a young girl who came every day to the small barrel-vaulted cement room, where, just beside the path, there once stood four apple trees. She would leave her shoes by the wooden door, painted green, and step onto the carpets that were thrown over the earthen floor. This girl was suffering from what doctors diagnosed as an incurable disease. Her great joy and strength came from visiting her beloved Baba. Each day she performed the same ceremony of removing her shoes, entering the tomb, bowing, and sitting beside the wooden sarcophagus that covered the earth and bones of Old Baba. The structure was horizontal and looked like a wooden man lying on his back. A soft green cloth was over its breast and a Mevlevi sheikh's *destar* (dervish hat) perched on its head. On the cloth, woven with faded yellow thread,

> "Allah, Allah" became every sound Rumi heard, and he began to whirl in ecstasy in the middle of the street.

63

were the words *"Ishq Allah Ma'abud l'illah"* (God is love, God is the one beloved, God is the act of love). Quietly sitting in meditation, the young girl tasted the sweetness of the moment and, as she left the space, ate the small amount of salt from the extended palm of the old man who tended the tomb.

After some time, the girl's illness vanished. Many attributed this to the salt from the tomb. She returned to the tomb every day of her adult life, grew into womanhood, and died an old person's natural death.

It is said that when she died, her flesh turned into the feathers of a peacock. From that day, Old Baba became known as *Tavus* (the peacock) Baba.

The Sufi poet Iqbal said, "Make Rumi thy guide in thy journey, that God may grant thee fire and warmth of human heart."

In Meram lived Mevlana's cook, Atesh Baz, a simple man who loved Mevlana from the depths of his being. He eagerly awaited those times when Mevlana journeyed the five miles up to the small village. One night it was announced that Mevlana was coming unexpectedly to Meram and wished to serve a great meal to all his mureeds.

On this particular night there was not enough wood to keep the fire. Rather than delay Mevlana's meal, Atesh Baz put his foot into the dying embers, causing flames to lick the side of his leg and catch onto the waiting logs. When he removed his foot only his big toe was burned badly, which to him was a sign that his faith was not perfect. When Mevlana arrived, Atesh put one foot over the other so that his sacrifice would not be noticed. Mevlana saw his position and understood what had happened. He embraced Atesh Baz, assembled the dervishes, and said, "Few on earth have such faith as Atesh Baz. In the future all our dervishes will bow with one foot placed over the big toe to remind them what faith really means."

These were difficult years for Mevlana. While he spoke of universal love and was the living example of his words, the Muslim states were being threatened by Mongol forces and Konya felt nature's wrath in the form of constant earthquakes. The Mongols captured Jerusalem and slaughtered thousands of Muslims.

Mevlana said, "If you grasp knowledge through the heart, it is a friend. If you limit it to the body alone, it is a snake."

In Konya, his mureeds grew in number. But, as it was with most great masters, only a few could really fathom his worth to the point of seeing themselves in the mirror of his heart and then breaking the mirror in order to remain with the essence of themselves.

To a few close mureeds Mevlana once referred to Mansur al Hallaj, saying, "He was killed, and his body dismembered by his own students and friends for saying *'Ana l' Haq'* [I am the Truth, I am God]; if I told what I knew, my body would be chopped into small pieces."

Remembrance
of Allah
satisfies hearts.

When it is found out that one knows the Truth, the payment is dear. For Shams it was his head. For Mevlana the mystic it was the knowledge that no one was prepared to receive his secret, and he would die with it still in his heart.

Once, in the tekke, a dervish complained that the door made a disturbing creaking sound whenever anyone came into the room. Mevlana looked at him and said, "The sound of a door opening is disturbing to you because all doors are closed to you. I love this sound, for all doors are open to me."

Mevlana would rise each morning before the call to morning prayer. One morning his wife came into his room and saw red clay on his shoes. This was not common to the terrain of Konya so she questioned him about it. Mevlana told her that during the night he went to Madinah to visit the Prophet. Everyone who is left far from his source wishes back the time when he was united with it.

In the years remaining before his death, verses poured from him as he walked the streets, in the garden, during the day or night, and Husam took down every word that came from his mouth. Later, he would read these notes to Mevlana, who would correct them and return them to Husam to be rewritten.

The task took years, interrupted only once for a period of fourteen months because of the grief Husam experienced at the death of his beloved wife. When the vast work was completed, the result was the greatest Muslim work since the Koran. It became known as the *Mathnawi,* the spiritual couplets of Mevlana Jalalu'ddin Muhammad er-Rumi.

On the surface it appeared as if Rumi co-mingled poetry and prose, but his importance is not confined to literature. He must be understood as a poet in the most exalted sense, one who gave expression to a situation lived with from birth. The yearning, the claw-like scraping of the inside of his chest, the emptiness, the fullness of his heart, the despair, the aloneness—these were the signs of his separation from the Beloved. He was the reed separated from its reedbed, that, in desperate aloneness, creates a wailing sound that emerges from the holes pierced in its heart.

Tugrel Inançer, the sheikh of the Halveti Jerrahi order today and a Mevlevi sheikh, described the esoteric meaning of the ney. "Music is uplifting to the listener. The ney (reed flute) has a system of seven holes, six are on the top of the instrument and one is at the bottom. These relate to the holes in the head of a person. The hole on the bottom is controlled by the thumb and is rarely opened. Melodies are mainly created by moving the fingers on the upper six holes. The bottom hole represents the mouth and is rarely opened indicating that the mouth should not always be open. The eyes, ears, and nose are frequently open. The nostrils are especially open so as to smell beautiful scents, particularly the fragrance of the Prophet Muhammad. To open the eyes is essential for good manners. To open one's ears is necessary to hear advice from a sage. Not to open your mouth on the other hand is good so as to hide one's ignorance, as well as keeping your immaturity hidden."

Rumi referred to the *Mathnawi* as "the shop for Unity and anything you see there except the One is an idol."

As his body aged, the cold, damp winters of Konya bit into his skin. Tiny icicles hung from the white hairs that were once the dark beard of his youth. Once, while in prayer, he wept so profusely that his beard, dampened by tears, froze, and icicles pasted it to the frigid ground. In the morning his mureeds found him in this position. As the winter of 1272 unfolded into spring, Mevlana felt a resurgence of physical energy. It was the dawn of his last year on the planet earth.

Sitting knee to knee in the zikr circle of the Mevlevis, Mevlana's voice called the *Asma'-Ullah-i-Ta'Ala* (the Attributes of Allah the Exalted) with a sound that seemed to arise from the core of a place where footsteps were unfamiliar. The shoulders of his cloak were threadbare from the constant rubbing with the dervishes standing on either side of him during the Muslim prayers, which he had done five times a day every day of his life.

The last summer in Meram was peaceful. His body became older, and his light-filled eyes and heart were at the peak of youth and maturity. He stepped, shoeless, onto the carpeted floor of the small semahane (ceremony room) and kissed the mouth of each of his dervishes with the palm of his hand as they bowed and knelt before him. He cleansed his body by fasting and meditation and spent long hours alone in the large garden. The yellowed walls of the garden were high and assured him the privacy of a thought or feeling. Autumn crowded summer in 1273, and October brought winter and frequent earthquakes. In November he became ill. News of his illness spread through Konya and its neighboring cities.

For forty days his family and friends showed grave concern. They were about to lose a guide to the unknown, a baraka (grace) from above. Many of them wondered whether they could have listened closer or worked harder in His service. They observed their laziness, their sense of superiority, and vowed that if he left them now, they would carry on his work.

Mevlana was not preparing for death, for he knew that with each breath, with each repetition of *"Allah Hu Akbar"* (God is great), he was moving closer to his Beloved.

> The lover visible
> And the Beloved invisible–
> Who ever saw such a love
> In all the world?

For Mevlana, the day of death was a time of "union," and he referred to it as the "wedding day" and sheb-i arus (the nuptial night).

Semazens in a posed 19th-century photograph. The Mevlevis have a tradition of boys participating in the sema.

Before he died Mevlana said:

> Do not search for me in the grave.
> Look for me in the hearts of learned men.

On the evening of December 17, 1273, Mevlana passed into "union" as the Konya sun burned bright red. The funeral was far from simple, but in its complexity and confusion it revealed the universality of Mevlana's teachings.

The day after his death, crowds filled the streets of Konya, waiting for the long procession that moved to the wailing sound of the ney. People of all races and religions shared in the shouldering of the coffin. There was shoving as people wedged themselves through the crowd and scrambled to touch the green cloth that covered Mevlana's coffin. It took the entire day for the coffin to move through the throng and arrive at the altar.

Mevlana's dear friend, Sadr al-Din al-Qunawi, was to have conducted the ceremony but he had fainted at the beginning of the procession, and Kadi Sirajeddin conducted the service. Mevlana was buried next to his father's huge, intricately-designed wooden sarcophagus, which now stands vertically in the Mevlevi tekke of Konya. The sarcophagus of Mevlana is covered with a large green cloth with borders and designs woven with golden thread. The *tawhid*, la illaha illa'llah (there is no god but God), appears on all sides of the cloth, woven with the same golden thread. The sarcophagus itself is covered with tiles. A large sheikh's hat with a green cloth wrapped around its bottom, almost forming a sphere, rests on the head of the sarcophagus. The entire room is filled with gold, and the walls are covered with tiles on which the names of Allah are inscribed.

Carved into the wooden sarcaphogus over the tomb of Rumi is this ghazal from the *Diwan-i Kabir*:

> Do not visit my tomb without *daf* (a circular drum played
> with the fingers, also called a *bendir* in Turkish)

One should not enter the banquet of God with sorrow.
And in the *Mathnawi* Rumi wrote:

> I died from a mineral, and plant became;
> Died from the plant and took a sentient frame;
> Died from the beast, and donned a human dress;
> When by my dying did I e'er grow less;
> Another time from manhood I must die
> To soar with angel-pinions through the sky.
> Midst Angels also I must lose my place,
> Since "Everything shall perish save His Face."

Let me be Naught! The harp-strings tell me plain
That unto Him do we return again.

After Mevlana's death, Chelebi Husam became the leader of the Mevlevi Order until he died in 1284. On Thursday nights there was a sema (whirling dance) in the semahane of the tekke (prayer lodge), which was adjacent to the mausoleum where Mevlana and his father were buried. Before the sema, each dervish went before Mevlana's tomb, bowed, and said a short prayer.

The tekke also contained dervish cells, a kitchen, a library, and a small mosque. The kitchen, which was a sacred place for the dervishes, was closed to the public when the tekke was turned into a museum in 1927. Mevlana's son, Sultan Veled, assumed leadership of the dervishes after Husam's death. He introduced the sheikh into the turning ceremony in honor of his father and teacher. Sultan Veled wrote treatises on his father's teachings and made the Mevlana Mausoleum the headquarters of the Mevlevis.

Following his death in 1312, Sultan Veled was succeeded by his son Ulu Arif Chelebi, who played a major role in the foundation and organization of the Mevlevi Order. When he died in 1320, his brother Shemseddin Emir Alim became the sheikh of the order. With his death in 1338, his sons and descendants carried on the position of sheikh.

By then, the Mevlevi Order had spread throughout Anatolia and beyond. The Mevlevi tekke in Konya was the largest of all the Centers and flourished as a school of art and culture for many centuries. Thirty-two *chelebis,* direct descendants of Mevlana, have occupied the position of sheikh of the order.

Turkish miniature of Mevlana. This early portrait is thought to be a good likeness of Rumi.
Opposite: Sheikh Selman sits on the red post representing the sun and Shams of Tabriz.

Look to the Source, if permanence you claim;
Go to the Root, if constancy's your aim.

…The gardens may flow with beauty
But let us go to the Gardener Himself.

Konya Sheikh Suleyman Loras

"If we do not strive
for inner perfection,
we will remain what we are now—
talking animals.
The world has never been
without teachers.
Each age has its teachers.
Jesus, Buddha, and Muhammad
were some of the
great ones, but there are
always qtubs, special beings
who take care of the world.
The perfect man,
the complete man,
lies within each of us."

The body is like the earth, the bones like mountains the brain like mines, the belly like the sea, the intestine like rivers, the nerves like brooks, the flesh like dust and mud. The hair on the body is like plants, the places where hair grows like fertile land and where there is no growth like saline soil. From its face to its feet, the body is like a populated state, its back like desolate regions, its front like the east, back the west, right the south, left the north. Its breath is like the wind, words like thunder, sounds like thunderbolts. Its laughter is like the light of noon, its tears like rain, its sadness like the darkness of night, and its sleep is like death as its awaking is like life. The days of its childhood are like spring, youth like summer, maturity like autumn, and old age like winter. Its motions and acts are like motions of stars and their rotation. Its birth and presence are like the rising of the stars, and its death and absence like their setting.

Preceding page: The tomb of Mevlana covered by a gold-embroidered cloth. Above: On the 700th anniversary of the "wedding night" of Mevlana, Istanbul Sheikh Selman Tuzon and Konya Sheikh Suleyman Loras shared the honor of the red post. Above right: Mevlevi music master Nezih Uzel in front of the ornately covered sarcophagi of Rumi's grandsons, just below and to the left of the sepulchre

of Rumi and his son Sultan Veled.
Left: The green-tiled fluted dome under which lies the tomb of Mevlana. Tiles with writing from the Koran and the *Mathnawi* form a band around the top of the dome.

Mehmet Susamish

Mehmet Susamish is eighty-two and has been turning in the Whirling Dervish Ceremony since he was fifteen years old. He is called Sivas Dede, after the city of Sivas, where he is a muezzin in the Ali Pasha Mosque. Five times each day he performs the *Adhan,* the call to prayer.

Allahu Akbar, Allahu Akbar,
Allahu Akbar, Allahu Akbar,
Ashhadu an la illaha illa'llah, Ashhadu an la illaha illa'llah,
Ashhadu anna Muhammadan Rasulu-llah.

The real goal in the sema is transformation, which can come when there is intention.

Ashhadu anna Muhammadan Rasulu-llah.

Hayya 'ala-sala, Hayya 'ala- sala. Hayya 'ala-l-falah. Hayya 'ala-l-falah.

Allahu Akbar. Allahu Akbar.

La illaha illa'llah.

God is great,

I bear witness that there is no god but God.

I bear witness that Muhammad is His Prophet.

Come to prayer.

Come to success.

God is great.

There is no god but God.

Rumi said: "Why art thou slumber-bound, like clay the earth caressing? In movement shall be found the key to every blessing."

Sema

The Whirling Dervish Ceremony
performed in The Hall of Celestial Sounds

Mevlana Jalalu'ddin Rumi was aware of the movement and sound in all of the planet. The sema (whirling dance) of the dervishes is an expression of the cosmic joy experienced by the simultaneous effect of annihilation and glorification.

Mevlana has described sema in many ways. "It is the witnessing of the state of perceiving the mysteries of God through the heavens of divinity.

"Sema is to fight with one's self, to flutter, struggle desperately like a half-slaughtered bird, bloodstained and covered with dust and dirt. It is to be aware of Jacob's grief and know its remedy; to know the vibration of meeting Joseph and the smell of his shirt.

"Sema is a secret. The Prophet Muhammad said, 'I have a time with God and during this time neither angel or prophet can intrude.' Sema is to attain that place where even an angel cannot go."

Today the tekke is closed. There is no organized Mevlevi Order of dervishes. The lovers of Mevlana participate in the yearly December sema in Konya, honoring the anniversary of Rumi's day of union. The *semazenbashi* (dance master of the Mevlevis) trains the new whirlers in the manner used in the old tekkes.

It is said that a true dervish is never bored, because he never does anything twice. Man continuously journeys around the circle of himself, repeating past actions and trapping himself in a net of his own creation. From the time the skull of Abel, the first man to die, was placed into the earth, man has buried the sacred; he has buried the maps to his freedom.

Plow your way through the crowds at the entrance to the gymnasium in Konya where the Mevlevis perform the sema. Avoid the arms of commerce

As he turns the semazen subvocally invokes the Name of Allah and empties himself of all that is not Him.

and the outstretched hands of the hawkers who sell everything from books and records to gold pins, cufflinks, and shoehorns with Mevlana's picture inscribed on them. Somewhere, buried beneath this external flash, this tourist glitter, can be found secrets of how to live.

> What I may not see, let me not see;
> What I may not hear, let me not hear;
> What I may not know, I ask not to know.
> Beloved, I am contented with both Thy speech and
> Thy silence.

The dervishes no longer walk through the doors of the three-hundred-year-old wooden tekkes and whirl barefoot on the mirror-smooth floors of the semahane. The Thursday night semas and zikr of the Mevlevis are past. The *Mukabele* meeting, "which brought a sense of deep peace and joy which everyone shared," has been reborn in Konya, the resting place of Mevlana. Like all that is reborn, the essence is manifested within a new structure. The place of worship has changed from a monastery to a high school gymnasium but the essence of the ceremony is much the same as it was for hundreds of years.

The English author, Jane Pardoe, gives a detailed description of her visit to the chapel of the Turning Dervishes in 1836.

"I paid two visits to the convent of Turning, or as they are commonly called in Europe, Dancing Dervishes, which is situated opposite the Petit Champs Des Morts, descending towards Galata. The court of the Tekie is entered by a handsomely ornamented gate and having passed it, you have the cemetery of the brethren on your left hand, and the gable of the main building on your right. As you arrive in front of the convent, the court widens, and in the midst stands a magnificent tree of great antiquity, carefully railed in; while you have on one side the elegant mausoleum in which repose the superiors of the order; and on the other the fountain of white marble, roofed in like an oratory, and enclosed on all its six sides from the weather, where the Dervishes perform their ablutions ere they enter the chapel. The mausoleum is of the octagon form, the floor being raised two steps in the centre, leaving a space all around, just sufficiently wide for one person to pass along. The sarcophagi are covered with plain clay-coloured cloth, and at the head of each tomb is placed the genlaf, or Dervishes hat, encircled by a clear Muslim handkerchief embroidered with tinted silks and gold thread.... Huge wax candles in plain clay-coloured candlesticks are scattered among the tombs.

"The chapel is an octagon building of moderate size, neatly painted in fresco. The centre of the floor is railed off, and the enclosure is sacred to the brotherhood; while the outer circle, covered with Indian matting, is appropriated to visitors. A deep gallery runs round six sides of the building, and beneath it, on your left hand as you enter, you remark the lattices through which the Turkish women witness the service. A narrow mat surrounds the circle within the railing and upon this the brethren kneel during the prayers; while the centre of the floor is so highly polished by the perpetual friction that it resembles a mirror and the boards are united by nails with heads as large as a shilling to prevent accidents to the feet of the Dervishes during their evolutions. A bar of iron descends octagonally from the centre of the domed roof, to which transverse bars are attached, bearing a large number of glass lamps of different colours and sizes; and against many of the pillars, of which I counted four and twenty, supporting the dome, are hung frames, within which are inscribed passages from the Prophet.

"Above the seat of the superior, the name of the founder of the Tekie is written in gold on a black ground in immense characters. This seat consists of a small carpet, above which is spread a crimson rug, and on this the worthy principal was squatted when we entered, in an ample cloak of Spanish brown, with large hanging sleeves, and his genlaf, or high hat of gray felt, encircled with a green shawl. I pitied him that his back was turned towards the glorious Bosphorus, that was distinctly seen through the four large windows at the extremity of the chapel, flashing in the light, with the slender minarets and lordly mosques of Stamboul gleaming out in the distance.

"One by one the Dervishes entered the chapel, bowing profoundly at the little gate of the enclosure, took their places on the mat and bending down, reverently kissed the ground; and then, folding their arms meekly on their breasts, remained buried in prayer, with their eyes closed and their bodies swaying slowly to and fro. They were all enveloped in wide cloaks of dark coloured cloth with pendant sleeves; and wore their genlafs, which they retained during the whole of the service.

"There was a deep stillness, broken only by the breath of prayer or the melancholy wailing of the muffled instruments, which seemed to send forth their voice of sadness from behind a cloud in sudued sorrowing, like the melodious plaint of angels over fallen mortality—the concentrated and pious self-forgetfulness of the community, who never once cast their eyes over the crowds that thronged their chapel.

"Immediately after passing with a solemn reverence, twice performed, the place of the High Priest (sheikh), who remained standing, the Dervishes spread their arms and commenced their revolving motion; the palm of the right hand being held upwards, and that of the left downwards. Their under dresses consisted of a jacket and petticoat of dark coloured cloth, that descended to their feet; the higher order of brethren being clad in green, and the others in brown, or a sort of yellowish gray; about their waists they wore girdles, edged with red, to which the right side of the jacket was closely fastened, while the left hung loose; their petticoats were of immense width

The longing sound of the ney permeates the semazens' hearts, transforming them into the ones who are not confined by boundaries. It is with this feeling that they re-enter the world.

85

and laid in large plaits, beneath the girdle, and, as the wearers swung around, formed a bell-like appearance; these latter garments are worn only during the ceremony, and are exchanged in summer for white ones of lighter material.

"The number of those who were 'on duty,' was nine; seven of them being men and the remaining two, mere boys, the youngest certainly not more than ten years old.... So true and unerring were their motions that, although the space which they occupied was somewhat circumscribed, they never once gained upon each other and for five minutes they continued twirling round and round, as though impelled by machinery, their pale passionless countenances perfectly immobile, their heads slightly declined towards the right shoulder, and their inflated garments creating a cold, sharp air in the chapel from the rapidity of their action. At the termination of that period, the name of the Prophet occurred in the chant, which had been unintermitted in the gallery; and, as they simultaneously paused, and, folding their hands upon their breasts, bent down in reverence at the sound, their ample garments wound about them at the sudden check. An interval of prayer followed; and the same ceremony performed three times."

Before entering the Hall of Celestial Sounds the dervish performs ablutions and prayer. Then he proceeds to dress in the whirling costume unique to the Mevlevis. His attire is influenced by the mourning clothes that Rumi ordered after the death of Shamsi Tabriz. The *sikke,* the tall honey-colored felt hat, represents the tombstone of man.

The desert Arab wears his shroud wrapped around his head. An old man was walking in the desert when he was approached by the angel of Death. "It is your time," said Death. "Let me at least go to the next village and purchase a new *galibiya* (long garment), for the one I wear is almost threadbare and if it takes months for my body to be discovered, I will surely be naked." Death gave him three days and the two agreed to meet in the same place. After the days passed the old man again appeared wearing a new galibiya, and Death took him. Some time did pass before the body was found by travellers and the galibiya he wore was tattered from the sun and wind. A large white cloth was wound around his head and they took that to wrap his body and then buried it in the desert. Since that time the Arabs wear an *emma* (a cloth wrapped at the head, their shroud) as a reminder that Death can come at any time.

The sikke of the Mevlevi is such a reminder.

The word *cemetery* comes from the Hindu word *samadh,* which denotes a permanent state. Holy men who died were set in a grave in a lotus *rishi* position, and a *lingam* was placed on the top of their heads.

The *tennure* (long white skirt) represents the shroud, and the *khirqa* (black cloak with long, large sleeves) symbolizes the tomb. Beneath the cloak the turner wears a *dasta gul* (literally, a bouquet of roses) and a white jacket, the right side of which is tied down; the left hangs open. Around his waist is fastened the *alif-lam-and* (girdle of cloth about four fingers wide and two and a half feet long). On his feet are soft leather slippers which are ankle high. He is now prepared to begin the ceremony.

The dervishes enter the semahane led by the semazenbashi (the dance master), and, slowly, with heads bowed, line up on one side of the hall. The dance master, who is closest to the sheikh's post, wears a white sikke. The sheikh is the last to enter the hall. He stops to bow at the axis line to his post and proceeds to walk slowly to the sheepskin dyed red to honor Shamsi Tabriz and represent the sun. The musicians are at the opposite end of the hall on a raised platform, facing the sheikh. The *hafiz*, who knows the entire Koran by memory, begins the ceremony by chanting a prayer to Mevlana and a sura from the Koran. Then the sound of the *kudum* (kettle drums) breaks the silence. The dervishes, now seated on their knees, listen to the piercing sound of a single ney, the reed flute which plays the *peshrev* or music prelude.

The semazen carefully ties the *kamer* (belt), which holds the *tennure* (shroud) in place, allowing for a bell-like appearance as he turns.

The dervishes slap the floor with their hands, indicating the day of the Last Judgment and the bridge Sirat that is crossed to get from this world to Paradise. It is said that this bridge is as thin as a hair and as sharp as a razor.

The sheikh takes one step to the front of his post and bows his head. He begins to walk slowly around the semahane followed by all of the dervishes. They circle the hall three times, stopping to bow to each other at the sheikh's post. As they bow they look between the eyebrows of the dervish opposite them and contemplate the divine manifestation within him. They know that every meeting is precious because every meeting contains a hidden farewell. The believer is a mirror to the believer.

This is known as Mukabele (to return an action) and has become the name for the Mevlevi ceremony. This part of the sema is known as the Sultan Veled Walk, in honor of Rumi's son, and symbolizes man's identity and his place within a circle. The *halka* (circle of dervishes) is a position used in many of the Sufi orders. The zikr circle is the living *mandala*.

After circling the hall for the third time, the last dervish bows to the post and turns to complete the walk as the sheikh takes his post. They now all bow and in one motion remove their cloaks, kiss them, and let them drop to the floor. As they drop their cloaks, they leave their tombs, their worldly attachments, and prepare to turn for God. The sheikh and the semazenbashi keep their cloaks. In the *Fihi Ma Fihi* Rumi tells us that: "If you sow a seed without its shell it will not sprout, but when you plant it in the ground along with its shell it will sprout into a great tree. Therefore the body too is of importance in principle, for without it neither can work be effected nor can the goal be reached."

So the semazen drops his black cloak, leaves the heaviness of his body, his worldly attachments, and turns toward his heart, his breath filling his hollowness with the Name of Allah. Then he returns to the body so that he may remain in the world.

The musicians on the platform are playing as the dervishes, with their right hand on their left shoulder and their left hand on their right shoulder (forming the name Hu in a mirror image), slowly walk to the sheikh's post. The semazenbashi is the first to arrive at the post where the sheikh is standing. He bows to the sheikh, his right foot over the left and his arms crossed at the shoulders. He kisses the right hand of the sheikh, recedes backwards from him, and, standing five feet from the post, is in a position to begin directing the sema.

Each dervish approaches the sheikh in this manner. He bows, kisses the right hand of the sheikh, the sheikh kisses his sikke, the dervish bows again and turns toward the semazenbashi for silent instruction. If the foot of the semazenbashi, who wears white shoes, is extended outside of his black cloak, it is a signal for the whirler that the outside area is blocked to him, and he must begin to turn on the inside of the dance master. If the dance master's shoe is hidden, the whirler continues to walk past him and begins to unfold and turn on his outside.

The Mevlevi sema offers a direction. Man wants the freedom of not being tied to a direction; therefore he is without direction and scattered. Recall the words of Sheikh Necmeddin: "When you are everywhere, you are nowhere, and when you are somewhere, you are everywhere." Each soul is guided by the heart. If you awake in the morning and genuinely ask for a spiritual guide, one is there.

Whirling and foot stamping is not only done in the Mevlevi sema but is shared by other Sufi orders. When the sheikh of the Halvetis begins a *devran,* circular movement in the zikr, he stamps his right foot indicating that the dust of the world is dispersed and one has control of the *nafs,* his lower self. Rumi said in the *Diwan-i Kabir*:

> Stamp under the feet, everything that is not Him,
> This is the way of reaching the Beloved.

All the dervishes unfold and whirl as the musicians play and the chorus chants. The turners extend their arms; the right palm faces up and the left down. The energy from above enters through the right palm, passes through the body, which is a visible channel, and, as this grace is universal, it passes through the left palm into the earth. With extended arms, the dervishes embrace God. As they turn, the dance master slowly walks among them gesturing with his eyes or position to correct their speed or posture. The sheikh stands at his post. They turn counterclockwise, repeating their inaudible zikr, "Allah, Allah."

At the conclusion of a selam, the semazen stops so abruptly that his billowing skirt wraps around him as he bows toward the post.

The semazen shifts his center of gravity, and when the center of gravity is shifted to the world of *malakout*, the spiritual world, by means of the zikr, one is also more present in the world of *mulk*, the world of duality, this world of choice, but in a different way. As one turns, orientation is lost; one loses one's grip on things. Intellect and action become one and existence is without boundaries.

After about ten minutes the music stops, and the dervishes complete a turn that will face them toward the sheikh's post and halt. The movement is so quick that their billowing skirts wrap around their legs as they bow to the post. They then step back in a line and begin the next selam.

This is repeated four times, each about the same duration. In the second, third, and fourth selams, a dervish who is tired may drop out and remain standing at the side as the others turn. It is only in the fourth selam that the sheikh joins the dervishes. He represents the sun; the dervishes are the planets, turning around him in the solar system of Mevlana. The sheikh whirls slowly along the equator line to the center of the semahane as a single ney sounds a distant wailing sound that leads him back to his post. He holds his khirqa (cloak) chest-high with his right hand and turns with measured steps, much in the manner that Rumi did before him.

Mevlevi music is not necessarily for listening–it is for participation. Hearing is in proportion to one's attraction. The Koran is protected–one who opens it and is not attracted will not see anything. Understanding lies in proportion to attraction. The moth is attracted to the flame; it circles the flame, motivated by the light, but only when it is burned, exhausted with the desire to know, does it understand the flame. The Mevlevi turns but only when he turns and is in complete exhaustion with the world (the state of non-resistance), constantly repeating the Name of Allah, constantly filling himself with the breath of that Name, can he experience Allah without the boundaries of the world. The sema itself is one of those boundaries.

The purpose of this life is to know Him. If one does not remain uneasy until the task of knowing the incomprehensible is fulfilled, then one is "like a bejeweled dagger which is stuck into the wall in order to hang an ordinary pot."

When the sheikh arrives at his post, he bows, sits on the post, and kisses the floor. All the turners sit, and their cloaks are placed on their shoulders by those who did not turn in the fourth selam. They have returned to their tombs but in an altered state. The sheikh recites the Fatihah, the first sura of the Koran, and all the dervishes kiss the floor and rise. The sheikh then sounds a prayer to Mevlana and Shamsi Tabriz and begins the sound "Hu." The dervishes join in sounding the "Hu," which represents all the names of God in one.

This concludes the ceremony, and the sheikh leads the dervishes from the semahane, stopping to bow opposite his post at the far side of the hall. Each dervish does the same.

On the night of December 17, in honor of Rumi's day of union with the Beloved, the ceremony concludes with the "greeting." All the musicians and turners line up and pass in front of the sheikh, kissing his hand. They kiss the hand of each dervish who has passed before them, leaving the last in line to kiss the right hand of about seventy of his brothers. It is a beautiful and touching moment that emphasizes the joy of the dervish when his thoughts turn to union with the Hidden.

It is not common for a dervish of another order to perform in the whirling ceremony, but the Mevlevis often bring their neys and bendirs (drums) to other tekkes where they join in the ceremony of that order.

Above: Contemporary Turkish miniature of a sema in a tekke. Painted by Ulker Erke. Opposite: Semazens turning during the sheb-i arus ceremony in Konya.

The semazenbashi of the Mevlevis and I went to the tekke of the Halveti dervishes in Istanbul. It was a cold winter Thursday night, and the Halvetis were about to begin their weekly ceremony under the leadership of a remarkable, universal being, Sheikh Muzaffer. We all sat in two concentric circles as Sheikh Muzaffer reached into the depths of his soul and brought forth the Halveti zikr, which carried the presence of God through each of us as we sat knee to knee in the three-hundred-year-old wooden structure. We repeated the zikr for about thirty minutes, aware of the pace and sound set by the sheikh. The vibrations of the breath of la illaha illa'llah filled the room and soon became the very air we inhaled. At the instructions of the sheikh we all rose, and two dervishes collected the sheepskins upon which we had been sitting and rolled up the carpets, leaving the bare wooden floor for our shoeless feet to move on. The two circles now became three with Sheikh Muzaffer choosing the inner circle. I was in the front when the Halveti sheikh invited the semazenbashi of the Whirling Dervishes to enter the inner circle and turn. We were all holding hands, turning clockwise, and sounding the heavy zikr *ya Hayy*. It was so cold in the tekke that our breath made patterns in the air.

There are things hidden and things revealed. Generally we see only the surface of things. The ear of a deaf person looks exactly like the hearing ear. So we know that hearing is hidden in the ear. The Mevlevi in their zikr do what appears to be a turning dance. But in fact as they turn toward their hearts they subvocally repeat the Name of Allah. Something happens within them that is hidden from the viewer. The totality of experience is in the world inside one's self and the world outside.

The semazenbashi slowly began to turn, his right hand holding the lapel of his overcoat, his long white beard touching his chest as he whirled with head bent and eyes closed. Here was the majesty of Mevlana. Here was the ecstasy of the dervish in the privacy of the tekke. Tears came to my eyes as I was carried in the whirling motion of the dervishes and the sound of the zikr. Men, whose names I did not know, embraced me and called me brother. Here in this small underground room was the key to inner peace. Here was the universal love that Mevlana lived.

May His blessings and His peace be upon them all.

Fahri Ozcakir

Fahri Ozcakir, the youngest of the turners, is twelve years old. His father, bottom left, also turns in the sema. "Sometimes, during the sema, it feels as if Mevlana is holding my hand. I begin to smile inside, and my heart is warm, and later it is as if what my eyes see is different from before."

Following page: At the conclusion of each selam the semazens stop turning, reform their line, and bow. Now they are ready to begin the next selam.

Rumi said: "Right sema is not for everybody, the fig is not the bait of every bird."

A congregation of sheikhs standing in front of the Mevlevi tekke in Konya in 1914.

Above left: The sheikh sits on his post, the semazens to his left, as the wailing sound of the ney penetrates the semahane.
Above: Detail of a dervish tekke in Turkey from a painting by Ulker Erke.
Following page: The sheikh slowly turns in the fourth selam while the semazenbashi makes certain his axis along a straight line from his post is clear.

"From love bitterness becomes sweet,
  from love copper becomes gold,
  from love the dregs become pure,
  from love pain becomes medicine,
  from love the dead become alive,
  from love the king is made a slave."

–Rumi

Enter the state of *wajd,* where one sees God in everything. In the state of wajd, a bliss that is coupled with a deep inner awareness of Allah, the Sufi may whirl, stamp on the ground, stretch out his arms (symbolizing an uplifting, an escape from the cage of the body), fall to his knees, or embrace the dervish next to him.
The tombstone of a Bektashi sheikh in Istanbul reads: "He has escaped."
Left: Detail of "Dancing Dervishes" (circa 1610)
Preceeding page: The call to prayer in the manner of Bilal, the first muezzin.
Following page: Often Mevlevis will visit the tekkes of other dervish orders. The heavy breath sound of the zikr enters the circle like a waft of sweet incense, as the visiting semazen turns, wearing his street clothes.

This rarely seen painting of a Rifa'i tekke in Istanbul was done by the Italian painter Fausto Zonaro in 1910. Zonaro loved the dervishes so much that he painted himself into the zikr line on the left. This is a typical tekke. On the right in the foreground is a hafiz, who is chanting a sura from the Koran; facing him is a visiting Mevlevi, who is playing the ney. There are two other Mevlevis, identifiable by their tall hats. Two visiting Rifa'i sheikhs are bowing as the sheikh of the tekke is about to walk on the backs of his dervishes in a healing ceremony. The children are brought to the front to view the healing practice. In the background are some English women. This is a composite image. It is unlikely that all these events would occur at the same time.

Zonaro must have painted two almost identical pictures as the one on the left (circa 1890) differs from the one above. Notice that the woman with a shawl about her head is not in the painting to the left. Missing in the painting above is the Mevlevi standing just behind the young girls and a boy who is just in front of the Mevlevi.

The hands in the painting above are not as well painted as on the earlier canvas. One begins to wonder if Zonaro actually painted both of them in what seems a twenty-year gap. If so, then why...perhaps an interested collector?

The Tekke

Being
The Divine Factory
of the
Whirling Dervishes

Above: *Allah Jameel,* Allah is Beautiful . . . loves Beauty. Left: Mevlevi Sheikh Suleyman Loras and his son Jalalu'ddin turn together at the Halveti tekke in Istanbul.

During Rumi's lifetime the sema (whirling dance) became the zikr for the Mevlevis. In the small semahanes (ceremony rooms) of Konya and Meram, Mevlana directed his mureeds to the path of ecstasy by means of this zikr in motion.

Later, as the semazens turned in the wide white skirts, which were their shrouds, and the tall tombstone-like hats, they experienced the joy that Mevlana embraced in front of the goldbeater's shop in Konya. In the garden in Meram, Rumi's followers turned slowly with him and were carried beyond the threshold. They soared above the cares and content of ordinary life.

In 1925 Kemal Ataturk passed a law which forbade these practices. The following was the initiation process of the Whirling Dervishes before that law.

The five Mevlevi tekkes, prior to 1925, were active dervish schools, which existed in communal fashion. Anyone under the age of eighteen was required to present written permission from his parents before he could be accepted to live in the tekke. The boy had to have a guide who was an older initiate in the tekke. The guide brought the boy to the sheikh of the tekke to whom he told his desire.

The sheikh initiated him with a ceremony consisting of the repetition of zikr (there is no god but God) and "Allah Hu Akbar" (God is great) and the presentation of the sikke (dervish hat) used in the ceremony. The mureed (initiate) was called upon to make a covenant of allegiance to the sheikh. In the West, discipline has come to indicate doing something contrary to one's comfort; in the tekke, discipline was learning while doing. It was being a true disciple. Obedience to the sheikh was not loss of one's freedom; through the preparation of "how to be" one gained one's freedom.

The initiate was given the choice of performing a chille (retreat) for 1001 days and then becoming a *dede* in the Mevlevi Order or becoming a *muhip* (an initiate who does not perform retreat and does not reside in the tekke, but comes every day for intense training in dervish practices).

If the choice was the retreat, the initiate was brought to the *ahchi* dede (*ahchi* means cook) and given his first test. The word *cook* in the Mevlevi Order had significance not only with regard to the preparation of food, but because man is raw material that has to be cooked into a dish that is edible. Those who were "raw" were men involved in the exterior side of life, while the "ripe" were men of the heart involved with the interiorization of self. The raw could not comprehend the state of the ripe.

Rumi said, "I was raw, then cooked, and now I am burnt."

The first test of the *nev-niyaz* (new young initiate) was to be brought to the *matbah* (kitchen), which was actually a small room where the initiate sat on his knees upon the *saka* (post, a sheepskin) for three days. Here he did not speak or sleep. He moved only to pray five times a day, to go to the toilet, and to eat the food brought to him. The *chillebesh* dede observed him to see if he was prepared to continue as a chille initiate.

On the fourth day the initiate was taken to the *hamam* (Turkish bath) to be bathed and shaved and given a chille *tennuresi* (a black dress) to wear throughout the retreat. He was brought back to the ahchi dede, who gave him a zikr to repeat while he performed his daily work.

At this time the initiate was turned over to the *kazandji* dede (*kazandji* means a large pot for cooking soup or *pilaw*) who became responsible for his education as a dervish. The kazandji dede oversaw the maintenance of the tekke and assigned the initiate to kitchen and cleaning duties. During the day the initiate also had to learn to be a semazen (whirler) and work with the semazenbashi (dance master). His days consisted of repeating his zikr, performing *namaz* (Muslim prayers) five times a day, doing service, and learning sema (dance). If it was his desire to become a musician, he had to gain the permission of both the ahchi and kazandji dedes. Training in the

The days of the Mevlevi initiate in the time of the tekke were spent learning sema, praying, training in music, studying the work of Rumi, and doing physical work such as cleaning and working in the kitchen.

ney began with the master asking the initiate to continually repeat Hu. As he did this, the master placed a ney close to the mouth of the initiate and a sound occured from the breath of the word Hu. This indicated to the initiate that when playing the ney he would become a living zikr.

The chille initiate was given a bed in the matbah, usually shared with two or three other young initiates. After the conclusion of the sunset prayers it was mandatory for the initiate to return to the main part of the tekke where he was trained in the *Mathnawi* or heard a discourse given by the sheikh.

If at any time he became a chille *kirmak* (one who has broken the retreat), he had to begin his chille again. The chille could be broken by any infringement of the rules of the tekke, disobedience, or failure to report to the main tekke for the evening class.

The chille initiate had first to complete the *muptedi mukabelesi* (the beginner's ceremony) before being allowed even to view the main sema performed every Thursday night. After learning the sema, it could be as long as a year before he graduated from the muptedi status.

His preparation in learning the Mevlevi turn was the same one used by initiates in the order since its inception. A smooth-surfaced board, three feet square and one inch high, is placed on the floor. In the center of the board is a large, smooth round-headed nail. Before each class and each sema, the whirler is required to perform *abdest* (ablutions). This is the washing of hands, mouth, nose, face, arms, head, ears, neck, and feet with cold running water while repeating the name of God. This is an important preparation for the sema.

The initiate kneels on the board and kisses the nail. He takes some salt, and, with his right elbow in his left palm and his left elbow resting on his left knee, he carefully places a small amount on the nail. He then rises and steps onto the board, placing the nail between the big toe of his left foot and the toe next to it. His right foot crosses his left at the toes. While his arms are crossed, right over left, at the shoulders, he bows his head and says *"eyvallah"* (with the permission of God). Now he is prepared to begin the lesson taught by the semazenbashi. Once he has learned the Turn, which usually takes ninety days, the initiate is given the muptedi status and can actually participate in a sema.

He learns that as he turns he fills his hollowness with the Name of Allah. When the first man was created the *shaytan* (devil) examined this new creation from the outside, then looked at the shape from the inside. The body was hollow. Here he moved freely and stated that this was a place he could work. The breath of the repetition of the Name of Allah fills the hollowness, leaving the shaytan no power over one who has filled himself with the breath of the divine sound of His Name.

The hadith states: "Allah, who cannot fit into the entire universe, can fit into the heart of a believer."

The remembrance of Allah fills that which is hollow, whether it is the reed or man.

If, when he first enters the tekke, the boy chooses to be a muhip (a lover), he lives at home but comes to the tekke every day, where he learns the sema, music, and is taught the *Mathnawi* by the different masters. He is also initiated with a sikke and is allowed to turn in the sema. Unlike the chille initiate, the muhip is allowed to view the Thursday night sema before completing the beginner's sema, which lasts until the dance master approves the perfection of his performance. In the Mevlevi Order today everyone is a muhip except Osman Dede, who is the only man alive to have completed the chille.

Upon completion of the 1001-day chille, the initiate was given a small room to himself where, for the next three days, he was brought food and sweets by other Mevlevis. He was now initiated as a dede in the Mevlevi Order and entitled to wear white garments.

After reaching the station of dede in the Mevlevis, the initiate was given the choice of remaining in the tekke or going to live in the city. If he chose to reside in the tekke he could not marry, because women were not permitted to live in the tekke. He was taken care of by the government, which gave money to support the tekkes. He functioned as a teacher and participated in the weekly sema.

If the initiate chose to live outside the tekke, he was allowed to marry and come to the tekke on Thursday nights, but he was under no obligation to do so.

On Thursday nights Mevlevi women were allowed to view the sema. Some would retire to another room and whirl without costume.

There have been women who were sheikhs in the Mevlevi Order. The most famous was Destine Hatun, the daughter of Sheikh Sultan Divani of the Afyon tekke.

Afyon, which means opium, is midway between Istanbul and Konya, and the tekke welcomed visitors going to and from the tomb of Mevlana. Mehmet Chelebi, a direct relation of Rumi and founder of the Galata tekke in Istanbul, is buried in the Afyon tekke. On his tomb is written, "Even if Jesus came to me, he could not cure me of the real sickness of my separation from God."

Sultan Divani was a great sheikh. When he died the post was given to his daughter, Destine Hatun, who wore a sikke and Mevlevi dress, and led the whirling dance in the semahane.

During the time that Destine Hatun held the sheikh's post, the tekke at Afyon burned to the ground. The community was poor and there seemed to be no way that the dervishes could rebuild. One night, before sleep, Destine Hatun asked for the help of her father. Sultan Divani appeared, dressed in his sheikh's robes, and told his daughter to go to a certain place near the stone fountain where the dervishes performed ablutions; there she would find a silver vessel filled with water. Destine was to pour out the water, and, when she reached into the vessel, her hand would emerge filled with gold coins, which would forever replace themselves in the vessel.

The following morning Destine went to the designated place, found the vessel and the gold, and began the reconstruction of the Afyon tekke. Whenever she needed money it was always waiting in the silver vessel.

There are seven main stations in the line of initiation in the Mevlevis. The highest is the sheikh of the order. Under him is the ahchi dede. Then comes the *neyzenbashi,* who is in charge of the ney players in the sema, and after him the *kudumzenbashi,* who leads the drum section. Equal in initiation to these last two is the semazenbashi, the dance master. The kazandji dede maintains the tekke and the *meydandji* dede acts as secretary to the sheikh.

Only those initiates who have gone through the chille are allowed to be initiated to these posts. If the sheikh wishes to initiate a Mevlevi to the station of neyzenbashi, he is first required to go to the Konya tekke where he is given a special eighteen-day chille under the direction of the ahchi dede of that tekke.

The sheikhs in all orders were chosen by a committee of three persons who form the *sheyhulislam,* the highest post in the religion. This committee is made up of one Mevlevi and initiates of two other dervish orders. When the decision refers to a Mevlevi, his name is given to the Konya chelebi (Sheikh of Konya who is a direct descendant of Rumi), and he makes the announcement. The Konya sheikh has the power to give the destar (sheikh's turban) to any initiate of the Mevlevi Order, whether he is muhip or dede.

This was the procedure of initiation in the Whirling Dervishes until 1925 when Kemal Ataturk introduced Law 677 into the Turkish Republic.

It was a December Saturday during the final turn of the last sema when the military police entered the Mevlevi tekke in Uskudar and ordered it closed. The quick barefoot steps of the dervishes squeaked to a halt on the mirror-smooth wooden floor of the semahane. The chief of police read the law which stated that performing dervish practices, holding meetings in the tekkes, the profession of tomb-keeping and the office of sheikh, and other dervish initiations were abolished and, as of the reading, against the law of the Republic.

The dervishes wept. Their once-billowing skirts hung limp, like the shrouds they represented. Their sikkes now tilted away from the sun and became weathered tombstones. Sheikh Ahmed Remzi Dede began to speak to the dervishes. He recalled another closing of the tekkes. It was during the reign of Sultan Murad IV, who feared that the dervishes and their practices could turn against him with a great power. Those close to his ear whispered of the strange occupations of these madhoubs (God-intoxicated men) and warned the Sultan of the danger their freedom held. All the tekkes were ordered closed and all dervish practices forbidden. The doors of the Mevlevi tekkes were bolted for eighteen years before their rusted hinges once more creaked the sema prelude. The tekkes were closed before, and they re-opened. Perhaps the day will come when these doors will again open.

The sheikh silently walked away to change into street clothes and the wordless dervishes filed behind him, their hardened feet sliding across the floor.

The police padlocked the entrance door, enclosing the vibrations of love and peace and the curious after-sound of bare feet turning sharply to an

Although Sultan Murad IV died in 1640 at the age of 27, his years as sultan vividly displayed his savage personality. It is no wonder that the dervishes quickly complied with his order to close the tekkes.
Murad IV was known to frequent the coffee-houses in disguise and execute on the spot anyone caught smoking, which was forbidden at the time.

unplayed ney. That night the people came and placed burning candles on the police lock.

Two years later, in the winter of 1927, Kemal Ataturk allowed the tomb of Mevlana to open as a museum, a place where the lovers of Mevlana could come. He reiterated that Turkey was a modern country, and a modern society has no time for dervish magic. He recalled that those who belonged to tekkes did nothing but sit. They paid no tax, were exempt from military service, and made it necessary to separate religion from government.

The dervish orders were abolished, but there remained a freedom of belief such that those who want to perform any rite may do so in private but not under the aegis of an organized religious body.

The Mevlevi tekkes never reopened, and it took thirty years before an alternate situation, which again allowed the dervishes to whirl, was agreed upon.

"If the tekke is closed, then you must become the tekke." It was with this thought that Sadettin Heper, the kudumzenbashi of the Yenikapi tekke in Istanbul in 1925, approached the Mayor of Konya twenty-eight years later and began arrangements for the Mevlevis to whirl again. With him was Halil Can, a well-known ney player, and together they initiated the talks that finally led to the open revival of the Whirling Dervishes. Halil was willing to accept the Mayor's proposal that it should not be a dervish ceremony but an occasion for the celebration of one of the great Turkish poets. Mr. Heper held out until it was agreed that the Koran could be recited during the ceremony. Kani Karaca, the great singer of the Koran, was contacted. Kani is a hafiz, a protector of the Koran, the title given to those who can recite the entire Koran by memory.

In December 1953, an audience was invited to the local cinema in Konya and witnessed the first authorized Mevlevi sema since the tekkes were closed. It was not much of a sema, with only three musicians, Halil Can and Ulvi Erguner playing ney and Sadettin Heper playing kudum. Kani Karaca chanted the Koran and two whirlers, Hulki Amil Chelebi and Abdul Baki, whirled in their street clothes to the wailing sound of the ney.

In 1954 it was the same. Note of the event was made by the Tourist Association of Konya and by 1955, although it was still held in the local cinema, the Sultan Veled Walk was introduced to the ceremony and tennure and sikkes were worn. The number of musicians and whirlers increased and Resuhi Baykara occupied the sheikh's post. Jalalu'ddin Chelebi was the semazenbashi.

By 1956 the sema moved to the library in Konya, and a ceremony was also performed in Ankara, the capital of Turkey. That year Mithat Bahari sat on the sheikh's post and Resuhi Baykara became a semazen.

During one of these first semas, the police observed that one of the older dervishes was praying as he turned. After the sema, they reminded Sadettin Heper that this sema was supposed to be for the tourists and not a real sema for dervishes.

"He is an old man," replied Mr. Heper. "He has no teeth and so his mouth moves up and down when he turns."

Another December the police were concerned that young boys were participating in the sema. "They will grow and become dervishes," claimed the authorities. It was explained that the young boys were only being taught the movements of the dance. They knew nothing of its true meaning.

By 1956, the Whirling Dervishes began to attract many people from different countries. The ceremony was moved from the small library floor to the high school gymnasium. Once again, Konya became a cultural center.

The next disturbing incident occurred in 1967. Resuhi Baykara shared the post with two other Mevlevi sheikhs. As the three sheikhs slowly walked to the post, a newspaper photographer followed them and snapped a photo close to Resuhi Baykara's face. Resuhi suddenly turned and shouted, "Go away!" There was a great commotion in the semahane. After the ceremony a spokesman for the Tourist Association of Konya came to the microphone and announced that Resuhi Baykara would no longer be allowed to participate in the sema.

Resuhi Baykara then broke from the Konya dervishes, claiming that it was not a real sema but a show for the tourists. Through his influence there is a secret organization of "floating skirts" in London who perform the sema wearing tennure and sikke. The whirlers are both men and women.

After the incident with the photographer, the dervishes went to the Tourist Association and said that interference from photographers or newsmen during the ceremony was not good.

"So you make a real sema! This is unloyal," replied the Association's representative. It was then explained that this kind of outside interference hindered the concentration of the musicians and dancers. The explanation was accepted.

The dervishes are capable of creating an invisible wall to block out all external interruptions. There may be no Mevlevi tekkes, but to the Mevlevis this is not a show—this is a real sema. Sometimes small semas are performed in the privacy of dervish homes.

Today, when upwards of 25,000 people come from all over the world each December to crowd the town of Konya and observe the Mevlevis whirl their sacred dance in honor of the "day of union" of their founder, Jalalu'ddin Rumi, the sema itself has the flavor of the days when dervishes turned barefoot in the semahanes of the old wooden tekkes. This is an important bridge-period for the Mevlevis. This authentic flavor has yet to become a full meal and to take its place in the preparation of a completely universal esoteric platform.

If the semazenbashi's foot protrudes beyond his cloak, the semazen knows the way is blocked and begins to unfold his arms and turn to the inside of the dance-master. If the foot is not visible, then he proceeds to turn on the outside.

Above: The Yenikapi tekke burning in 1961.

LAW 677

WHICH PROHIBITS AND ABOLISHES THE PROFESSION OF TOMB-KEEPING, THE ASSIGNING OF MYSTICAL NAMES, AND THE OPENING OF TEKKES (DERVISH LODGES), ZAVIYES (CENTRAL DERVISH LODGES), AND TOMBS.
13 December 1925 (1341 H.)

Clause 1. All the tekkes (dervish lodges) and zaviyes (central dervish lodges) in the Turkish republic, either in the form of wakf (religious foundations) or under the personal property right of its sheikh or established in any other way, are closed. The right of property and possession of their owners continue. Those used as mosques and mescits (small mosques) may be retained as such.

All of the orders using descriptions as sheikh, dervish, disciple, dedelik (a kind of sheikh of an order), chelebilik (title of the leader of the Mevlevi order), seyyitlik (a descendant of the Prophet Muhammad), babalik (elder of a religious order, a kind of sheikh), emirlik (descendant of the Prophet Muhammad), nakiplik (warden of a religious order), halifelik (deputy sheikh), faldjilik (fortune teller), buyudjuluk (witchcraft), ufurukchuluk (a person who claims to cure by means of the breath), divining, and giving written charms in order to make someone reach their desire: service to these titles, and the wearing of dervish costume, are prohibited. The tombs of the sultans, the tombs of the dervish orders are closed, and the profession of tomb-keeping is abolished. Those who open the closed tekkes (dervish lodges) or zaviyes (central dervish lodges), or the tombs, and those who re-establish them or those who give temporary places to the orders or people who are called by any of the mystical names mentioned above or those who serve them, will be sentenced to at least three months in prison and will be fined at least fifty Turkish liras.

Clause 2. This law is effective immediately.

Clause 3. The cabinet is charged with its implementation.

Clockwise: The unfurling tennure, representing the shroud of the semazen, reveals the sheikh standing just in front of his red post.

The joy of a lover of Mevlana can be seen in the face of the shoemaker who makes the turning slippers for the Mevlevis in Konya.

In a little shop on Muze Caddesi, behind the Mevlana Museum, Ali Sapmaz forms the tall honey-colored wool sikkes (hats) for the dervishes.

125

Above left: Aka Gunduz, ney, Nezih Uzel, bendir, and kudumzenbashi Sadettin Heper are aware of the movements of the semazens. The semazens are also aware of the pace of the singers in the sema. As one does not go quicker or slower than the Imam in the Muslim prayer, so the semazen is guided by the sound of the singers.
The intent of the listener makes the music sacred.
Left: 19th-century photo of a ney player.

Music

by Nezih Uzel

It is not ordinary music,
this dervish music, it is music
you drink with your whole body,
your whole being,
and you live this music.

"The body of music is
a masterpiece from
the treasure of the
love of man."
The discs on this page,
from a rare book on
music published in
1852, represent the
modes and their styles.

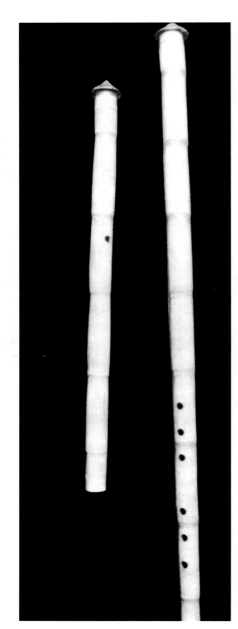

Above: Two of the six types of ney, which make different sounds according to their length.
Above right: The Mevlevi kudum is a small double drum played with two sticks. It has a deep sound like a soulful heartbeat.
Below: The bendir, played with the fingers.

NOTES FROM THE BOOK OF LIBERATION
(Kitab-el Necat)

There are two kinds of songs (*sharki*), those that are sacred and those that are profane. The first are remote from worldly things and exhort the listener to thoughts of the future life. They are usually written in verse and spoken in a litanic manner. The words can be realistic or allegorical but the intentions of the author must be pure and good or they will be lifeless and empty. Profane songs are full of lies and absurdities. Previously they had been allowed, but now they are forbidden.

With his mind on material goods, how can a man totally live? Inspired people have mastered their passions and have given their lives to their God. Their words and actions are divine, and they exalt and give life to those who witness them. It is like the command of the Creator to live. The spirit of the inspired word is divine and can create new life for those who see or hear them and take them to heart. Just as food gives physical strength, the divine word gives moral strength, but without inspiration the words are empty.

Those who speak without purity cannot animate our hearts. Their voices lack warmth. They can never uplift our souls. Only the frivolous and unworthy will hear their message.

All the foregoing is for the initiates. Those that are past this stage have greater insight. They can see the hidden truth in the allegories. With open hearts, they will become enchanted and wise.

It is true that our prophet Muhammad never sang songs, but he did listen –an indication that he accepted songs.

Songs stir the emotions and should be sung by someone with a good voice. (The same applies to verse reading.) The Prophet said, "Ornament the Koran by your voice." One day he told Abu Musa, one of the Koran singers, that he had David's flute in his throat. All of the prophets had good names, beautiful faces, and nice voices.

More recently Halveti Sheikh Muzaffer reminds us that to whirl in worship is one of the fundamental practices of Sufi orders.

> You will see the angels encircling the Throne,
> praising and glorifying their Lord.
>
> –Koran, Sura al-Zumar/75

"It is clearly to be understood from this noble Koranic verse," said Sheikh Muzaffer, "that the angels revolve around the Exalted Throne as they glorify their Lord. Just as the ritual prayers Muslims perform are modeled on the acts of worship of angels, so does the noble whirling ritual evolved by the Sufis reflect the worship of the angels of the Exalted Throne, for it is seen as a circling just like theirs in Remembrance of Truth."

ISMAIL HAKKI

Ismail Hakki (1653–1725), the author of *Kitab-el Necat*, was born in Aydos, a small village near Edirne. He lived so long in the city of Bursa that he is called "Bursai Ismail Hakki" (Ismail Hakki from Bursa). His masterpieces greatly influenced the literature and art of the Ottomans. He had a profound knowledge of grammar, rhetoric, logic, Islamic lore, and theology. Among his important works is *Commentary of Mesnevi*. Like many philosophers of the Middle Ages, Ismail Hakki composed music. According to him, a man of virtue feels the harmony of the universe within his soul through music. He was especially critical of those musicians who composed using only the intellect without being in harmony with their souls.

MEVLANA AND MUSIC

The teaching of Mevlana depends upon and is expressed in three elements: dance, music, and love. In his works, Mevlana admires music and accepts it as high art. According to him, music begins where speech ends, and it has the ability to contain and expose what words are unable to. The language of music is universal. It is the language of lovers.

During Mevlana's time, *rebab* music was often heard in Konya. Some of the upright men of the city criticized Mevlana's attitude toward it. Seyyid Sherefeddin said, "I also listen to the rebab music but I can't hear the 'heaven music' as Jalalu'ddin calls it, and I understand none of it." Mevlana replied that we hear the opening of heaven's door but that poor Sherefeddin hears only its closing.

The music that Mevlana approved of was what Ismail Hakki of Bursa called "concentration music." As one listens, he concentrates on the love of God. Because of this, it is also called "wisdom music." Its first two instruments are the rebab and the ney. In this music the ney is the symbol of man. In *Mathnawi*, Mevlana's great masterpiece (25,700 verses), he examines symbolization. According to him, the ney suffers from the separation from God that ends at death.

> Listen to the reed how it tells a tale, complaining of separations.
> Saying, "Ever since I was parted from the reed-bed, my lament hath caused man and woman to moan.
> I want a bosom torn by severance, that I may unfold (to such a one) the pain of love-desire.

THE FUNDAMENTALS OF MEVLEVI MUSIC

We do not have much information about the Mevlevi music during Mevlana's lifetime, but we do sometimes find the names and information about the musicians in the chronicles of Mevlana's period. In Mevlana's poems there is also information on musical techniques. In Mevlevi music, which has been known for centuries and improved upon continually, rhythm and voice are important, with melody assisting them both. These three elements work together in such a way as to create a monotonous music, which is the basic goal of Mevlevi music. Rhythm and voice must be connected during the flow, but basically they are independent. The rhythm instrument can create music of its own, just as the voice can. Melody unites them as an outer shell. This monotonous music takes the attention of men and guides it toward meditation. As we concentrate on the music we become one with ourselves and new insights are experienced.

Wisdom grows, which is the purpose of the music. We don't enjoy the music, but it makes us reflect. It may bore us, but it will also improve us. Mevlevi music isn't for listening; it is for participation. Through the knowledge of Mevlana and his teachings, we join in the ceremony by playing an instrument or by dancing. It must be remembered that all three elements–music, dance, and oneness with Mevlana–are essential to the ceremony. A missing element spoils the holiness and makes the ceremony pointless.

Master ney player Ulve Erguner whose sons Kudsi and Suleyman have kept the family musical tradition alive.

THE ORIGINS OF MEVLEVI MUSIC

Mevlevi music began with Mevlana. It is the music he favored; it is the music made by his beloved followers and it is also Asian music. Mevlana was Asian and the place one lives has an effect on one's entire life, on all one's behavior. Whether one plays or listens makes little difference, for the music reflects the soul. In Mevlevi music, we feel the enthusiasm and energy of the Asian mountains as well as the dignity and serenity of the plains. In the beginning, music was not for enjoyment but was a medium for the transmittal of Mevlana's words and thoughts, as it was also for Pythagoras, Homer, and Orpheus.

THE TECHNIQUES OF MEVLEVI MUSIC

Mevlevi music is a part of Turkish religious music, which in turn is a part of Turkish classical music. Turkish religious music has two main branches. The first is the music of the mosque; the second is mystical music, of which Mevlevi music is a part.

Mevlevi ceremonies are carefully composed structures. These ceremonies are divided into four parts, each of which is called selam (salutation). Each is connected through singing. In the first and second selams, selections from Mevlana's *Diwan-i Kabir* or *Mathnawi* are sung. In the third, the poems of other Mevlevi poets can also be sung.

Religious music and mystical music are played in different ways. Mystical Mevlevi music has different styles within itself. The music is generally directed by the chief drummer (kudumzenbashi). He is responsible for the flow of the music and decides whether it is to be played rapidly or slowly. The mystical atmosphere in the ceremony room influences his decision even though he, himself, dictates the relationship between the music and the dance. Whether the room is quiet or static is felt by the kudumzenbashi, and he will apply this influence to the music. It is important to note that the kudumzenbashi probably is not aware of being influenced because of his concentration on the ceremony. As we have mentioned, high concentration brings unawareness and thus spontaneity.

Although the variations of the parts and the rhythms are predetermined and the kudumzenbashi is responsible only for the speed of the music, it is enough for him to determine the spiritual tension of the ceremony.

NEYZENBASHI (CHIEF NEY PLAYER)

Another important element in Mevlevi music is the voice. The voice is first evoked by the ney because its music is very similar in sound to the human voice. The ney is used as an instrument in non-religious classical music as well, but when it is used in Mevlevi music it is more solemn and heavier. The ney players are directed by the neyzenbashi during the Mevlevi ceremony. Classical Turkish music has many kinds of *makams* or modes, and the Mevlevi ceremonies are composed in many different makams. Each ceremony is named after the name of the makam of which it is composed. The neyzenbashi makes a long improvisation to each makam, which is called a *taksim*. Sometimes he will give this duty to one of the neyzens. This improvisation depends on the mystical feelings of the neyzenbashi or the taksim player. He remembers the composed melody they are going to play and is influenced by the atmosphere of the room in much the same way as the kudumzenbashi. The participants of the ceremony reach the very first step of concentration with this taksim.

The ney itself is merely a dead piece of wood with seven holes cut into it. The ney comes alive from the breath of the ney player as he repeats the Name of God.

AYINHANLAR (THE SINGERS)

Most of the ceremony is oral. The words are the poetry of Mevlana and other thirteenth-century poets. Since the language of that century was Persian, the singers, to perform well, should have some knowledge of Persian. The selected poems are generally lyric, and in this way the music, rhythm, and poetry unite to construct the music of wisdom. The words, and even the syllables, of the poetry should be connected to the musical sentences. The words should be understood clearly–that is, the melody should not dominate the words, which have deeper meanings. In this way, the characteristics of Mevlevi music come through.

THE PARTS OF THE CEREMONY

The ceremony is divided into two parts. The first part is composed of the *Naat* (a poem praising the Prophet Muhammad), the ney improvisation (taksim), and the Cycle of Sultan Veled. The second part is composed of four selams, the final instrumental music, the recitation of Koran, and prayer.

The First Part
a. Naat. A form in religious music. The Naat, in Mevlevi music, was composed by Buhuriz Mustafa Itri (1640–1712), but the poetry belongs to Mevlana. (Turkish musicians often refer to the Rast makam as the basis of musical theory.) Naat is translated as follows:

O Lord Mevlana, friend of truth,
Thou art the most beloved of God.
Prophet without equal of the Creator,
Thou art the pure Being whom God has chosen among His creatures.
O my friend and Sultan,
Thou art the well-beloved of the Eternal,
Perfect and most exalted Being of the universe,
Thou art the Chosen among the prophets and the light of our eye.
O Mevlana, friend of truth!
O my friend and Sultan,
Messenger of God,
Thou knowest how weak and defenceless are thy people.
Thou art the guide of the powerless and the humble in spirit,
Freed of truth, my Sultan,
Thou art the cypress in the garden of the prophets,
Thou art the spring season in the world of knowledge,
Thou art the hyacinth and the rose-tree in the garden of prophets,
Thou art a nightingale of the world above,
Shamsi Tabriz has praised the glory of the Prophet,
Thou art the Purified, the Chosen, imposing and great, O thou, who curest
    the heart,
Friend of God!

Naat, which is without rhythm, is sung in a litanic style by one of the *ayinhans,* who stands while singing.
b. Taksim. The taksim, which we discussed earlier, is the most creative part of the Mevlevi ceremony.
c. The Cycle of Sultan Veled. This was contributed to the ceremony by Mevlana's son, Sultan Veled. During this cycle, the dervishes who take part in whirling walk around the semahane (the ceremonial room) three times and salute each other in front of the post. In this way they transmit secrets to each other.

The music played at this time is instrumental and is called peshrev. Peshrev is a well-known form of music, usually consisting of four parts with long rhythmic patterns, and is played at the beginning of a classical musical performance. The music of the peshrev is generally by the composer of the ceremony. This goes on until the Cycle of Sultan Veled is finished. The rhythm of the Sultan Veled Cycle is called the grand cycle *(Devr-i Kebir)*. The musical sentences of 56/4 rhythm are the longest rhythmic sentences used in Mevlevi music. This rhythm creates the effect of the music although it is played without voice. At the end of the Cycle of Sultan Veled another improvisation of ney is played, and the second part of the ceremony begins.

The Second Part
The Four Selams
a. The first selam. The melodies are usually long. The rhythm used is called the walking cycle *(Devr-i Revan)*. Its beats are 14/8. Occasionally a rhythm called *duyek* (two-to-one) is used.
b. The second selam. The rhythmic pattern of this selam is called *Evfer* and is composed of 9/8 beats.
c. The third selam. This is divided into two parts including melody and rhythm. The cycle in the first part is called the cycle, but it is different from the one used in the Sultan Veled Cycle. Its beats are 28/4. The second part of this third selam is in *Yoruk Semai* (a kind of waltz) and its beats are 6/8. There is a transitional rhythm between the two called *Aksak Semai* (limping waltz), and its pattern consists of 10/8 beats.

The fastest part of the Mevlevi ceremony is the last part of the third selam. The waltz rhythm used (6/8) in this part gives possibility of wider leeway to the composer. The performance of this part presents the opportunity for the highest mystical joys to be felt and expressed. Here, the mystical feelings have reached the summit and are transformed into ecstasy. The bond between the semazens and the musicians has become complete.
d. The fourth selam. The rhythmic pattern is again Evfer (9/8). The Evfer rhythm is slow and long and the previous ecstasy is reduced. Whoever became delirious during 6/8 beats begins to concentrate again.

Final Instrumental Music

With the end of the fourth selam the oral part is finished. The last peshrev is the finale, and it is in 4/4 patterns. The second Yuruk Semai in 6/8 patterns is the end of the ceremony. After this instrumental section there is a ney taksim. Sometimes this music can be played by stringed instruments.

Reciting of the Koran and Praying

After the music finishes, a hafiz from among the singers recites from the Koran. The sema continues till the Koran begins. When the hafiz begins his recitation, the semazens suddenly stop and step back to the edges of the room and sit down. The hafiz chooses the text he likes. After he finishes, the semazenbashi stands up and begins to pray in front of his sheikh. The prayer is a long one. Before 1923 the prayer was for the health and the life of the sultan. After the establishment of the Turkish Republic, the prayer was for the health of the founders and rulers of the republic. (This was ended in 1925 when the tekkes and tariqas were outlawed.) The prayer also is for Mevlana and all the holy men of the Mevlevi Order, who are mentioned by name. After the prayer is finished, everybody stands up. The sheikh reads a kind of prayer called *Gulbang* which finishes with the word Hu (meaning God). The entire group says Hu together. After this, the sheikh goes forward a few steps and salutes the semazenbashi; the semazenbashi returns the salute. During this salutation, both of them hold their voices in the same tone and extend the salutation for a few seconds. After this, the sheikh takes a few more steps and repeats the process with the neyzenbashi. Afterward, the sheikh leaves the semahane and the ceremony is over.

Ilahis, which were sung by all Sufi tariqas, were shared by many tariqas. The same ilahis that the Halvetis used in their zikr ceremony could also be heard in the Rifa'i or Kadiri gatherings.

THE COMPOSERS

ISMAIL DEDE

Ismail Dede created a new musical school as well as changing the appearance of the classical Turkish music of the nineteenth century. (Hundreds of his non-religious works are still played throughout the world.) He lived in Istanbul where he was born in 1777. He died in Makkah in 1845. Because his father was a bathkeeper, he was called *Hamamizade* (the son of the bathkeeper). His musical ability was so evident and his voice so clear that on the first day of elementary school he was chosen as the chief of the school chorus.

In the dervish registry of the Yenikapi dervish lodge, it is recorded that Dede first participated in the lodge when he was twenty-one (1798). He completed his chille of 1001 days and was accepted as a dede (a dervish who has completed the chille). During this time he also learned to whirl. Ismail Dede became famous after he began composing songs. He was invited to the Sultan's palace by Selim III.

With seven Mevlevi compositions to his credit, Dede was the composer of the largest number of Mevlevi ceremonies. He also wrote mosque music and music for other sects. Dede was a disciplined composer who turned his ability to the creation of new forms only after he had mastered the old techniques of composition.

Accordingly, classical Turkish music is divided in two parts, that before Dede and that after him. At the end of the Middle Ages, Eastern music was characteristically introverted. Dede turned this around, causing a reform like the Renaissance in Eastern music. This renaissance put an end to the music of the Middle Ages and created new fundamentals. Some music scholars have criticized Dede for having destroyed what was good in ancient music, but in reality what he was trying to do was to make music accessible to the greatest number of people.

Dervish music, as we have noted earlier, is wisdom music. Ismail Dede changed the form of reaching that wisdom. The seven ceremonies he composed are entirely different from those of Nayi Osman Dede. In some of them Ismail Dede, for the sake of art, went beyond the rules. For example, in the *Neva* ceremony the music is joyful and glorious. The dervish leaves his gloomy, spiritual room and walks in the fields collecting flowers. These revolutionary ideas should not necessarily be attacked because they are different. It is, after all, a way to commune with God.

The old music was abstract. The new had new instruments of expression, and because it was concrete it became routine. The work of Ismail Dede was a crucial moment in dervish music. Although he is admired for the radical change he brought about in music, the work being done in modern musicology is giving us the opportunity to know and appreciate that which came before. We respect Dede but we should also know the Mevlevi music that preceded him.

NAYI OSMAN DEDE

Turkish music started in central Asia and was continued in Anatolia, particularly among the lower classes. High class and Mevlevi music were heavily influenced by Arabic and Persian music. Starting in the eighteenth century, they began to come under Western influence. The last representative of the pure Asiatic-Ottoman culture was Nayi Osman Dede. Nayi Osman Dede is the first instructor of the third period in Mevlevi music.

In Osman Dede's great masterpieces the influences of the glorious ages of the Middle East can easily be seen. In his melodies, wisdom and music blend together and complete one another.

In 1672 he was appointed sheikh of the Galata dervish lodge. Gavsi Dede, the sheikh of the same *Dergah*, had previously been his teacher. The researchers who mention Osman Dede in their works claim that Dede's knowledge of sophos was inherited from Gavsi Dede. Osman Dede learned to play ney at the dervish lodge. During his education he became such a skillful and famous player he was called *Nayi*, which means ney-player. He composed four great Mevlevi ceremonies. These are called *Rast, Chargah, Usshak,* and *Hidjaz.* The third one, Usshak, was played in the 1973 Konya ceremonies. All of these compositions have the required length and are accepted as the premier works of the original Mevlevi music. Fortunately these four ceremonies were written in musical notes in 1936 by a group of musicians at the Conservatory in Istanbul.

Before Osman Dede there were five Mevlevi ceremonies. The first three– *Penchgah, Dugah,* and *Huseyni*–were composed very early, and their composers are unknown. The fourth composition, by Kochek Dervish Mustafa Dede, who died in 1683, is called *Beyati*. The fifth, *Segah*, was composed by Mustafa Itri, who died in 1711. Together with the four compositions of Nayi Osman Dede, these are the fundamental masterpieces of Mevlevi music.

After he had been the sheikh of the Galata dervish lodge (Mevlevihane) for eighteen years, Osman Dede composed a poem about the ascension of Prophet Muhammad. This music and poetry is still occasionally read in the mosques of Istanbul. It takes about three hours to perform and is so much of its age that only a few people know its composition.

Osman Dede has also composed valuable instrumental music. As well as being a composer and ney player, Osman Dede was a calligrapher. His tomb is near the door of the semahane at the Galata Mevlevihanesi.

SELIM III

Another Mevlevi composer was Selim III (1761–1808), an Ottoman Sultan. He became the sultan in 1789 at the age of twenty-eight and was killed during an internal crisis of the empire.

Selim was a gifted poet and musician. During the serious upheavals of the country, he purified his soul by creating works of art. He is responsible for one Mevlevi ceremony *(Suzi Dilara)* as well as several non-religious musical works.

Being a musician himself, Selim III was protective of musicians and artists with the result that many fine works were created. But this was also the time when the Ottoman-Turkish culture was influenced by the West, and so Turkish art changed. This was the time of Napoleon and the battles between the British and the French over the route to India that proved ruinous to the Ottoman empire. The days of glory were over. The rich cultural heritage was gradually forgotten and replaced by something new and facile.

Selim III was a Mevlevi follower and spent much of his time in the Galata dervish lodge. He often observed the ceremonies.

Because he was a Sultan, Selim's *Suzi Dilara* ceremony was not accepted in his time although it was truly valuable. Up to this period, Mevlevi ceremonies were growing in number and Selim's ceremony is the sixteenth that is known and sung.

The Ottoman sultans proved themselves in battle, and Selim III was no different. His personality was torn by the great upheavals during his rule, and he found solace in composing Mevlevi music.

AHMET AVNI KONUK

One of the last Mevlevi composers, Ahmet Avni Konuk was born in Istanbul in 1873. Although he lived after Ismail Dede, he mastered musical characteristics of the ages before Dede. Ahmet Avni graduated from law school and possessed great knowledge and culture in music. He composed several works of religious and non-religious music. The sophos culture which was inspired by the Sufi masters of ancient times is reflected in all of his religious works.

Ahmet Avni Konuk composed three Mevlevi ceremonies, all of which are in the classical form of the period before Dede.

Ruy-i Irak, a mode composition, was played in Konya in 1964 and was recorded live by Bernard Mauguin. (This record was issued by UNESCO.) Ahmet Avni Konuk did not have any knowledge of musical notes. (All of his works had been written by notists, but it must be remembered that to record the notes in Western musical forms is impossible.) The ancient music was transmitted from teacher to pupil. Avni Bey preserved this tradition through his musical education and in his composition. If the ancient music survives, Avni Bey will be responsible.

THE INSTRUMENTS

KUDUM

The kudum, a small double drum, is used for rhythm in Mevlevi music and played with drumsticks. There are three types of kudum: the kudum used for folk music, the one used in military bands, and the kudum used for mystical or wisdom music. In Anatolian folklore, the kudum is called *Chifte Na'ra* (double shout), and its metallic cup is sometimes made of earth.

The military kudum is called *Chifte Nekkare*, and its cup is always copper. In mystical music the kudum is a holy instrument, but in military music it is a sign of independence. The leader who commands Chifte Nekkare to be played in his military band is declaring independence for his nation or sect. It is not unknown for kudums to be attached to flags during battles.

The kudums used in mystical or wisdom music are of two varieties: the Rifa'i kudum and the Mevlevi kudum.

The Rifa'i kudum is one of three instruments of a musical group. (The other two are a cymbal [*Halile*] and *Mazhar* which is a tambourine-like instrument consisting of a wooden circle with skin stretched on it.) The Rifa'i kudum is a one-piece instrument, which is played with a skin belt instead of drumsticks. Its metallic cup is always brass.

The Mevlevi kudum is played with double sticks called *Zahme* and its metallic cup is made of copper that has been forged with a hammer. Camel or sheepskin is used to cover the top of this drum as well as for the strings that tie the skin tightly to the body. After this skin is tied to the body of the kudum, a skin cover is placed on the cup. Between the cup and this cover a *kitik* (a kind of stuffing) is placed. The skin is stretched on the cup in a hamam (Turkish bath). The stretching lasts for a few days, at which point the skin has loosened. After the skin and strings have dried, the skin is stretched tightly for the last time after the strings have been retied. The dried skin and the copper cup with the stuffing around it give this kudum its deep sound that is much akin to a soulful heartbeat.

The Rifa'is play their kudums when they are standing, holding them on their left arm while playing with their right hand. But the Mevlevis sit on the floor and place two kudums, which make different sounds, in front of their knees. The copper and the skin of the one on the right side are thicker than the one on the left and thereby produce a lower tone. Theoretically, there must be a difference of four notes between the two kudums; if the right gives an F sound, the left must give a B. To keep the kudum in position, a solid circular skin pillow is placed underneath each kudum.

REBAB

The rebab is an ancient Oriental violin that is still popular in the East. It was first used in the Middle Ages by the Turks, who called it *Iklig*. A hair taken from a horse's tail is tied to an arrow and is played with a bow rather than a pick. In the oldest sources it is noted that the rebab is made from a coconut shell that is covered by animal skin. It has quite a long handle and two horsetail hairs are strung close together.

The difference in the sounds of the hairs should be five musical notes. In some parts of Central Asia rebabs with curved horse's heads have been recorded. These probably reflect the importance of the horse in Central Asian mythology.

A dictionary written in 1403 includes the following description of a classical rebab: a bearskin stretched on a coconut shell. The handle must be made of hard wood, either ebony or almond will do. One of the horsetail hairs must be denser than the other.

Because the traditional rebab was difficult to play, the instrument was modernized at the beginning of the century with the substitution of metallic strings. Unfortunately, metal strings cannot reproduce the warm sounds of the horsetail strings, and consequently the followers of Mevlana do not accept the new rebabs. (The metallic-stringed rebab is suitable for brisk melodies and rhythms and for a new sound of its own.) In Mevlevi music the sound is more important than the melody, and because of its expressive sound the traditional rebab lends itself to the highest mystical experience.

In one of his masterpieces, Mevlana states that the sound of the rebab breaks the lungs of the man who listens to it. The *alif*-like strings indicate a union with the alif in the name of Allah.

Like the ney, the rebab is but a silent instrument until it is stroked by the fingers of the musician. Only then can its sound touch a note in the heart of the listener.

This sound encourages the semazen to enter a state of union with the Beloved, and with outstretched arms he expresses the joy of conquering his lower tendencies.

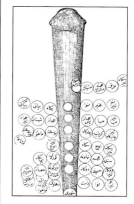

Voice schedule of the ney (rim-blown reed flute).

NEY

The plaintive sound of the ney (rim-blown reed flute) is an important instrument in the Mevlevi ceremony. This melodic instrument and its meditative mournful tone has been a symbol of yearning in Islamic poetry for centuries. Without the breath of the player the ney is but a dead piece of wood. With the breath of the sound of Hu the ney becomes alive and expresses its longing for its Creator with a sonorous wailing sound.

OTHER INSTRUMENTS

Stringed instruments are generally used in Mevlevi ceremonies (with the notable addition of the ney). The *kanun* (a zither-like instrument with seventy-two strings), the *tambur* (an ancient form of the lute still used in music that is non-religious), and the *ut* (a lute-like instrument with six pairs of strings played with a pick) can be used during the sema. In the early nineteenth century a piano was used in the Galata Mevlevihanesi in Istanbul, but the results were not considered suitable for Mevlevi music, and so the experiment was not repeated. In 1970, in a ceremony in Istanbul, a violin-cello was tried and found to be in tune with Mevlevi music, and in 1973 it became an instrument that could be used in the ceremony.

THE SOUND OF THE DANCE

The Mevlevi movements could have originated with the Pythagorian schools, which performed certain dances or "movements" in which each person turned to the ratio of the particular planet in the universe that he represented. Although the Whirling Dervishes do represent the planets, it is unlikely that the esoteric information of the Pythagorians has been passed on to those who turn today.

**In the 1970s a violin-cello was used in the sema ceremony and found to be compatible with the music.
Right: The music indicates to the semazens when to cease whirling and come to an abrupt stop while bowing to the sheikh's post.**

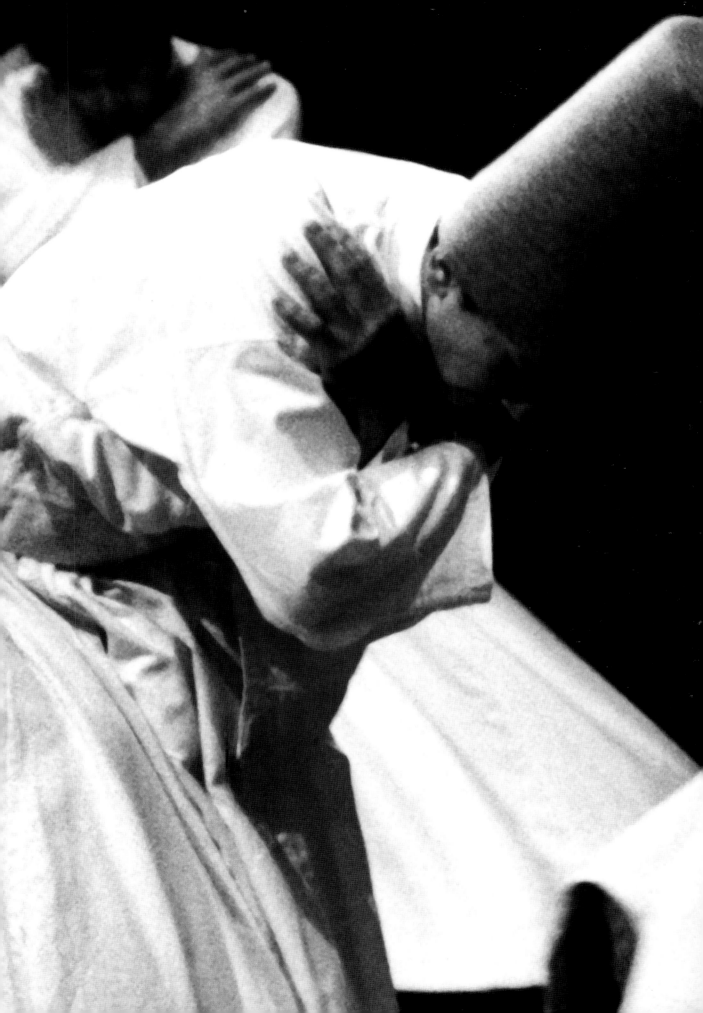

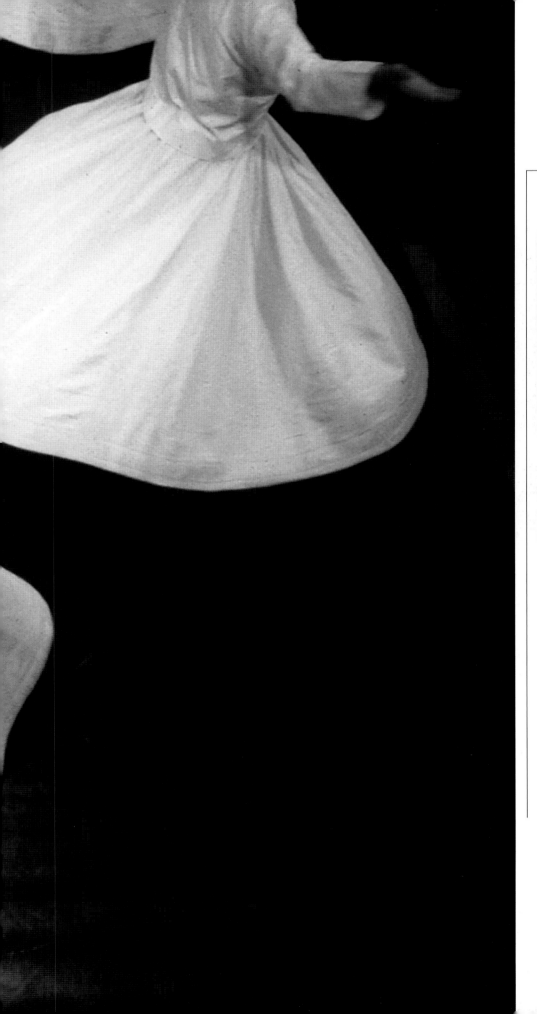

Through sema one can find one's soul, and the gates to a hundred gardens open.

Mevlevis bow before the sheikh as they proceed to begin turning.
Above: Early photograph of a ney player and a hafiz of the Koran.

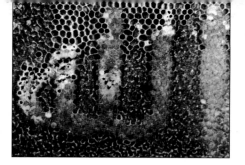

The Honey of His Counsel

The claims of the various countries and cultural groups who call Mevlana their own have little to do with the reality of who he was and to whom he belongs. Those who claim him do so based on the level of their percipience. All are blocked by their own images.

Mevlana said,

> The nation of love differs from all others
> Lovers bear allegiance to no nation or sect.

He was a bearer of love and a unifier of those who saw separation. One can continually argue whether he was a Turk who spoke Persian or an Afghan born to Arab lineage and in this discussion lose the essence of Mevlana's teaching, the cultivation of conscious impressions manifesting as a brotherhood of all mankind based on love.

Although predominantly Muslim-Turkish, Konya's population included Christians, Jews, Greeks, and Armenians. It was an ideal place for the "teacher of brotherly love" to reside. But one should not forget that Rumi was a Muslim, a lover of the Prophet Muhammad, who accepted people of all religions to his circle of knowledge. Mevlana referred to Konya as "the Makkah of the heart," and wrote:

> If you seek to soar to heaven, make friends with all men.
> Never harbor a grudge in your heart.
> The joy of friendship is Paradise.
> When you talk of enemies, thorns and snakes fill your heart.

He wrote (dictated) in Persian and influenced all those who read the language. As a "living holy man" his abode was Anatolia, but his mark has been left in all of Turkey, Iran, and now a good part of the Western world. His influence was great, and among his disciples were theologians, lawyers, men of government, and, in the late eighteenth and nineteenth centuries,

Above: A devout Muslim bee-keeper found this honeycomb in one of his bee-hives, in the village of Karakoy, Turkey. In the formation of the honeycomb the bees have written in large and clear letters the most beautiful name of the essence of God: Allah.
And Allah says in the holy Koran (Sura al Nahl, The Bee, 68/69): And thy Lord revealed to the bee: make your honeycomb in the mountains and in the trees and in the hives which men build, and eat all the flowers and fruits and do in the way of thy Lord submissively. There comes forth from their bellies a liquid of many hues, in which there is healing for men. Therein is surely a sign for men who reflect.

sultans who were all proud to "look upon him."

In the garden of his *khalifet* Husamaddin in Meram, Rumi gave sohbets (spiritual discourses) on deep subjects to a circle of listeners. Later these talks were collected and became the *Fihi Ma Fihi (In It Is What Is in It)*.

"Each person's spirit will return to his body, in the same way that awareness returns to the body in the morning. At night everyone goes to sleep– shoemaker, king, judge, tailor and all the rest. Their thoughts fly away from them, and no thoughts remain for anyone. Morning breaks and gives life to the motes of their bodies. The thought of each one is like a scroll; flying and running it returns to each. There are never any mistakes. The tailor's thought returns to the tailor, the lawyer's thought to the lawyer, the iron-monger's thought to the ironmonger, the tyrant's thought to the tyrant, and the just man's thought to the just man. Does anyone go to bed a tailor and wake up a shoemaker? No, for that activity and occupation belong to him, and once again he occupies himself with it. So you should know that in the next world it is the same way. This is not impossible, for it happens in this world."

The real sheikh is not always easy to find. "Every walnut is round," said Rumi, "but every round thing is not a walnut."

"Every tongue is a curtain over the heart. When the curtain is moved, the mysteries hidden behind it are revealed. The tongue is like the lid of a cooking-pot; when it is moved, you know what sort of food is inside. One whose sense of smell is keen can tell by the vapor issuing from the closed pot whether it is a pot of sweetmeat or sour stew flavored with vinegar. Even if the oral explanation is false, yet the scent, the impression produced by the speaker, makes one acquainted with his veracity or his falsehood."

If one is blind and deaf, then the door to the world of sight and hearing is closed. But a man can be blind and deaf in his understanding. If this be the case, then the inner world, the secret world, the world of the unseen is closed to that man.

Listen to Rumi's story of the grammarian and the boatman. A grammarian embarked on a boat in order to cross the Bosphorus. It was late at night and the only boat gliding on the sea was small, and rowed by one man with a set of oars.

Halfway to shore the grammarian, an arrogant fellow, asked the boatman, "Have you ever studied grammar?" "No," he replied. His passenger said, "Then half your life has been wasted."

The boatman was heart-broken with grief but remained silent. A short time later the wind forced the small boat into a whirlpool. The boatman shouted to the grammarian, "Do you know how to swim?" "No," he answered. "O grammarian," said the boatman, "then your whole life has been wasted because the boat is sinking in these whirlpools."

If you cannot swim in the ocean of life, no matter what you think you know, you will surely drown.

There is the story of Mullah Nasreddin. He lost his house key and was dilligently looking for it under a streetlamp. A neighbor observed him and asked what he was doing. "I'm looking for my key," answered the Mullah. "Is this where you lost it?" asked the neighbor. "No, I lost it over there by the door to my house, but it is dark there so I am looking for it here where there is more light."

Religion is with Allah in the world of the unseen. The signs of Allah are in the world of the seen, but Allah is in the world of the unseen. The signs are on the horizon, but the secrets are within. Rumi says that it is necessary to look for a thing where it is.

Dr. Abdulbaki Golpinarli, Turkish scholar and author of many books on Mevlana, reveals to us that "Mevlana never came to terms with the important people of his time but embraced the people, while his son, Sultan Veled, confined his humanist ideology, which was capable of spreading to all mankind, to piety, making it the property of a single community and deepened its mysticism."

After Mevlana's death the Mevlevi Order spread to all parts of the Ottoman Empire. Tekkes were established, and the cultural and moral influence of this "urban" order of Sufis expanded into government procedure. Dr. Golpinarli stated that "the Mevlevi tekkes were like universities of their time." They influenced Turkey through the arts of calligraphy, music, and literature. Through the centuries Turkish poets have been magnetized by the essence of Mevlana's teaching.

The poverty of our time is spiritual amnesia. But man has always needed a reminder, such as a word or phrase, or at times a garment. The cloak of the dervish is always large. It never shrinks; one must grow into it.

The Prophet Muhammad once offered his cloak to any one of his companions who could pray two *rekaats* (cycles of prayer) without his thoughts going astray. One man said he would attempt to do it. Just as he approached the end of the second rekaat he thought, "I wonder which cloak the Prophet will give me."

One must reach out for the "rope of Love." In earlier days, after a particularly spiritual sema, when semazens embraced the state of *wajd* and *jezbeh*, the sheikh would have all the tennures and cloaks worn in the sema placed on the floor of the semahane. They were then cut into small pieces and given to the semazens and musicians as "fragments of baraka." The fragments gathered from several sema ceremonies would be sewn and patched to make a cloak referred to as *morrakka* (patched), which was worn as a blessed garment.

When one is in a high spiritual state, fragments of energy emerge from the body and permeate the clothes one wears. Worn later, they can be a reminder of the state of remembrance. This is why the same clothes or woolen shawl are often worn in meditation, and a particular kind of vest is worn in the zikr of the Halveti dervishes. The room in which one meditates, prays, and repeats the Name of Allah takes on a presence which is built up by these practices.

Faith in Allah is the real cloak of the dervish. It is his protection from the onslaught of negative events woven into each day.

155

Rumi once gave his cloak to someone who provided him with dubious information about the whereabouts of Shams. He said, "I have given my cloak for a lie. I would have given my life for the truth."

Each year in Makkah, the *kiswa* (cloth which covers the Ka'ba) is cut into small pieces and given to the people, as a reminder, by the Custodian of the Two Holy Mosques.

Another reminder in the sema and the zikr of many dervish orders is the stamping of the right foot, lifting one from one's lower self to a state of preparation. In an early biography of Rumi, Aflaki wrote that Mevlana would begin the sema by stamping his right foot to the ground and shouting *Hayy* (The Alive; the One who is all-knowing and His strength is sufficient for everything).

Today Mevlana's thoughts are being heard in the West where a rebirth of an understanding of Rumi is occurring. The tekkes are closed. The Mevlevi sheikhs who knew Mesnevi, Koran, and the Persian language are no more. No one knows the sweet taste of the *Gharib Sema*, the secret sema performed after the sema, in the privacy of the tekke, by the sheikhs and dervishes with no onlookers.

When the tekkes are closed, then the dervishes must become tekkes. Today what is important is to disseminate the ideas of Mevlana Jalalu'ddin Rumi.

There is less concern about his planetary origin, and many are applying the teaching to daily life.

> Come, whoever you are,
> Whatever your belief,
> Come, and eat the honey of his counsel.

The Phoenix

The great Sufi master Faridu'd-Din'Attar relates the tale of the Phoenix–a wonderful bird found in India. It has no mate and dwells in solitude. Its beak is long and hard, like a flute, and contains nearly one hundred holes. Each hole sounds a different tone, and each tone reveals a mystery. A philosopher-friend of the bird taught it the art of music.

When the Phoenix utters these sounds, all the birds of the sky and fish of the sea are affected and the wild beasts are made silent by the entrancing music and experience of ecstasy.

The Phoenix lives about a thousand years. It knows the time of its death, and when this knowledge is tearing at its heart, it gathers a hundred trees, heaps them in one spot, and begins a fire. It then places itself in the middle of the fire. Through each of the holes in its beak it sounds a plaintive cry; out of the depths of its soul it utters its dying lament, and then begins to tremble.

At the sound of the music all the birds gather. The wild beasts assemble to be present at the death of the Phoenix. At this time they all become aware of their own death. When the moment arrives for it to draw its last breath, the Phoenix spreads its tail and feathers. With these it kindles a fire that spreads swiftly to the wood-pile and begins to blaze. Soon the fire and bird become one red-hot mass. When the glowing charcoal is reduced to ashes and only one spark remains, a new Phoenix arises into life.

GLOSSARY

Author's note: As the Turkish, Arabic, and Persian languages are difficult for most Westerners to pronounce I have taken the liberty of mixing them to ease the reader. For example, Mevlana Jalalu'ddin is Turkish and Persian but seems phonetically better for Western readers than Mevlana Celaleddin, usually only seen in Turkey.

ABDUL QADIR GILANI ('Abd al-Kadir al-Djilani) (or al-Djili) Muhyi al-Din Abu Hanbalite theologian, hafiz, and Sufi, who gave his name to the order of the Kadiriyya. b. 470/1077–8; d. 561/1166. Considered to be the greatest Saint of Islam. Was Persian from Nayt (Nif) in Djilan, south of the Caspian Sea. He went to Baghdad to study at age eighteen and remained there until his death. He first appeared in public as a preacher at age fifty (520/1127). Received *khirqa*, the Sufi robe, from al-Mukharrimi.

ABDUR RAHMAN JAMI (Mawlana Nur al-Din 'Abd al-Rahman Djami)
Great Persian poet of mysticism. b. in Khadjird, in district of Djam on 23 Sha 'ban 817/7 November 1414; d. at Harat on 18 Muharram 898/9 November 1492.

ADHAN
"Announcement," a technical term for the call to divine service of Friday and the five daily prayers in Islam.

ABU HAMID AL-GHAZZALI (1058–1111)
Theologian, logician, jurist, and mystic, he was born and died at the town of Tus in Central Asia. Most of his life was spent lecturing in Baghdad or following the path of a wandering dervish. His writings are a bridge between Sufism and traditional Islam.

AHMED AL-GHAZZALI (Ahmad B. Muhammad al Ghazali)
Brother of the more renowned Abu Hamid al-Ghazali, the Sufi and popular preacher. He made his way to Baghdad and took his brother's place when the latter retired from teaching at the Nizamiyya. He died in Kazwin in 520/1126.

BAQA (Baka' wa Fana)
The Sufi terms *fana* (passing away, effacement) and *baka* (subsistence, survival) refer to the stages of the development of the mystic in the path of gnosis.

BURAQ (al-Burak)
The mythical horse on which Muhammad is said to have ridden when he made his miraculous "night-journey" from Makkah to a remote place of worship (possibly a point in the heavens).

CHILLE
A retreat. In the Mevlevi tekke, the retreat was for 1001 days.

DERGAH (Dargah)
Persian, literally "place of a door." Usually "royal court" (but in India with the additional specialized sense "tomb" or shrine of a *pir*). The tekke, or congregation place of the dervishes.

DERVISH (darwish, darwesh)
Commonly explained as derived from Persian and meaning "seeking doors."

FANA
The passing away of all things, including himself, from the consciousness of the mystic, and even the absence of the consciousness of this passing away and its replacement by a pure consciousness of God.

FARID AL-DIN 'ATTAR ('Attar, Farid al-Din Muhammad B. Ibrahim)
Persian Sufi poet. Dates of his birth and death are not certain, but it is believed that he was born on 540/1145 and killed as a result of the Mongol destruction of Nishapur in 1221.

FIKR
"reflection," "meditation"
In the performance of *fikr*, the Sufi, concentrating upon a religious subject, meditates according to a certain progression of ideas on a series of evocations which he assimilates and experiences. In fikr, concentrating on the subject recollected–generally a Divine Name–he allows his consciousness to lose itself in that object, thus the importance granted the technique of repetition.

HAFIZ
Protector of the Koran. One who knows the entire Koran by memory.

HALVETI
The secluded dervishes.

HIJRA (hidjra) (Latinized as hegira)
The emigration of Muhammad from Makkah to Madinah in 622. The word connotes the breaking of ties of kinship or association.
(Muslim dates are normally given according to the era of the *hidjra*. This era does not begin on the date of Muhammad's arrival at Madinah, but on the first day of the lunar year in which that event took place, 16 July 622.)

JALALU'DDIN RUMI (CELALEDDIN) (Djalal al-Din Rumi)
B. Baha al-Din Sultan Al-'Ulama Walad
B. Husayn B. Ahmad Khatibi, known by the sobriquet Mawlana (Mevlana).
Persian poet and founder of the Mawlawiyya (Mevlevi) Order of dervishes, which was named for him.
Born 30 September 1207 near Balkh; died 17 December 1273 in Konya.

KA'BA (Ka'bah)
The physical center of Islam, situated almost in the center of the great mosque of Makkah. The stone house built by Abraham and his son Ishmael. The direction of prayer for all Muslims.

The name is connected with the cube-like appearance of the building. It is, however, only like a cube at first impression: in reality the plan is that of an irregular rectangle. The northeast wall, in which the door is (the front of the *Ka'ba*), and the opposite wall are 40 feet long; the two other walls are about 35 feet long. The height is 50 feet. Built of gray stone, it stands on a marble base 10 inches high. Four lines drawn from the center through the four corners roughly indicate the four points of the compass.

KONYA (ancient Inconium)
A town in Asia Minor on the railway from Baghdad, the capital of the province of the same name.

Formerly the capital of the Seldjuks of Rum, whose monuments still survive. The city in Turkey where Rumi lived, taught, and is buried.

KORAN (al-Qur'an)
The sacred book of Islam, containing the collected revelations of the Prophet
Muhammad as revealed over a period of twenty-three years.

MADHOUB (madjhub)
"attracted"
In Sufi terminology, denotes a person who is drawn by Divine attraction *(djadhba)*
so that without trouble or effort on his part he attains a union with God. In other
words, the *madjhub* experiences the ecstatic rapture of losing himself in God and is
thereby distinguished from the *salik* (traveler) who makes the journey to God, stage
by stage, with conscious endeavor and purpose.

MADINAH (Medina)
From the Arabic *madinah*, "town."
A town in Arabia, the residence of the Prophet Muhammad after the hidjra, from
622–632. The capital of the Arab empire under the first caliphs. The real Arabic
name of the city was Yathrib (Jathrippa).

MAHMUD SHABISTARI
A Persian sage of the thirteenth century. Little is known of his life. His writings
include *The Secret Garden*, a Sufi classic.

MANSUR AL-HALLAJ (Al-Halladj)
Al-Halladj (the wool-carder) Abu' L-Mughith al-Husayn B. Mansur B. Mahamma
al-Baydawi.
Arabic-speaking mystic theologian (244/857–309/922). His life, his teaching, and
his death throw light on a crucial period in the history of Muslim culture; the interior experience which he describes can be considered a turning point in the history
of *tasawwuf.*
  Born in Tur, he had learned the Koran by heart at age twelve. At twenty he
received his Sufi cloak from 'Amr Makki. He was executed/martyred 22 March 922.
His last words are purported to be, "All that matters for the ecstatic is that the
Unique should reduce him to Unity."

MATHNAWI, MESNEVI
In Persian, Turkish, and Urdu, poetic compositions of any length dealing with epic,
romantic, ethical, or didactic themes are of this form, which probably originated in
Persia.
  This form was used by Djalal al-Din Rumi in his *Mathnawi.*

MAKKAH (Mecca)
Birthplace of the Prophet Muhammad. Each year millions of Muslims make a
pilgrimage to Makkah, called the *Hajj.*

MEDRESE
A school for religious learning.

MEVLEVI (Mawlawiya, Mewlewi)
Order of dervishes called by Europeans Dancing or Whirling Dervishes.
Name derived from *mawlana* (our master), a title given to Rumi.

MUEZZIN
He who "calls to prayer" the Muslims, five times each day. Bilal, an Abyssinian
devotee of the Prophet Muhammad, was the first *muezzin.*

MUHAMMAD

The founder of Islam (the holy Koran was revealed directly to him), native of Makkah, known as the Prophet of Islam (The Seal of the Prophets).

MUHYI-D-DIN IBN 'ARABI (Muhyi'l-Din)

Ibn al-Arabi, Muhyi'l-Din Aby 'Abd Allah Muhammad B. 'Ali B. Muhammad B. Al 'Arabi al Hatimi al-ta'I, known as a *Shaykh al-Akhbar* (the greatest sheikh), (560/1165–638/1240), was one of the leading Sufis of Islam. Born in Seville, Spain.

MUKABELE

A meeting. A common name for the Mevlevi ceremony.

MUPTEDI

A station in the Mevlevi order of one who is a "lover of Mevlana" but has not gone through the three-year retreat (*chille*) in the tekke.

MUREED (murid)

"Novice": the term applied during the period of preparation to one who wishes to enter a dervish order (*tariqa*), a devotee.

MUSLIM, MOSLEM

A believer of Islam. One who follows the five pillars of Islam and the Hadith of the Prophet Muhammad.

NAQSHIBENDI (Nakshbandi)

An order found by Muhammad B. Muhammad Baha al-Din Al-Bukhari (717/1317–791/1389). *Nakshbandi*: "Painter" or "drawing incomparable pictures of the Divine Science" or more mystically "holding the form of real perfection in the heart." Involved with the mystery of symbols.

QTUB, KUTUB

Literally "axes" (pl. axis) or "poles."
In theological and mystical language, *al-kutb* is the name of the holiest of saints, who, however, is unknown to the world.

RABIA OF BASRA (Rabi'a Al-Adawiya)

A mystic and saint of Basra, a freewoman of the Al 'Atik, a tribe of Kais. B. 'Adi, known also as al-Kaisiya, born 95 (713–714) or 99; died and was buried at Basra 185 (801). A few verses of hers are recorded; she is mentioned and her teachings quoted by most of the Sufi writers and the biographers of the saints. Famed for her teachings on mystic love, she led a life of extreme asceticism and otherworldliness. She was stolen as a child and sold into slavery. Upon gaining her freedom, she retired to a life of seclusion and celibacy, first in the desert and then in Basra.

SA'DI (Sheikh Muslih-al-Din)

His renown is second to that of no Persian poet. Was born at Shiraz in 580/1184 and died there in September 1292. He is buried in the environs of that city.

Best-known works: *Bustan* (Garden), written in 1257, and the *Gulistan* (Rose Garden), written in 1258. The former is a collection of poems on ethical subjects and the latter a collection of moral stories in prose, plentifully interspersed with verse. He is regarded as a master of the short ode (*ghazal*).

Well-versed in mystical "science," he may even have met Rumi.

SADR AL-DIN AL –QUNAWI (Qunawi; Konevi)
Stepson of Ibn-'Arabi. Passed on the 'Arabi lineage to Mevlana.

SALAT (namaz, *Turkish*)
Arabic name for ritual prayer or divine service. The highest goal of the *salat* is
complete absorption in Allah. It is referred to as the greatest *zikr.* Performed at
specific times, five times daily by Muslims.

SELAM (salam)
Used as a substantive in the meaning of "peace, health, salutation, greeting."
Frequently used in the Koran as a form of salutation.
  Also: a litany which is pronounced from minarets every Friday about half an hour
before the beginning of the midday adhan.
  Also: blessings of the Prophet which are sung from the minarets during the month
of Ramadan about an hour after midnight.

SEMA (sama)
In Sufism: listening to music, singing, chanting, and measured recitation in order to
produce religious emotion and ecstasy (*wajd*) and such performances by voice or
instrument. A meditation, a remembrance, not an entertainment. The Whirling
Dance of the Mevlevis.

SEMAZEN
A whirler in the *sema.*

SEMAZENBASHI
The dance master of the Mevlevis.

SEYYID
One directly in the lineage of the Prophet Muhammad.

SHAMSI TABRIZ (Tibrizi, commonly called Shamsi Tibrizi.
Shams al-Din Muhammad B. 'Ali B. Malikdad-I Tabrizi).
A Sufi, the spiritual guide of Rumi, who composed in his name the greater part of
the collection of mystical odes known as the *Diwan-i Shams Tabriz (Divani Shamsi
Tabriz).* Born in Tabriz, arrived Konya in 1244, and vanished mysteriously as a
result of the jealousy of the students of Rumi.

SHEIKH JUNAYD (Abu-l Qasim al-Junayd ibn Muhammad)
Born (birthdate unrecorded, possibly 215AH) and raised in Baghdad in a family of
merchants. Studied law and hadith, known as a great Sufi master. Died 298AH (910).

SIKKE
The dervish hat worn in the Mevlevi sema. Tall and honey-colored, made of wool,
and represents a tombstone.

SILSILAH (silsila)
"Chain of the order." Lineage of a Sufi order going back to the Prophet Muhammad.

SURA
Chapter of the Koran.

TARIQA (Tarika)
The way. The path of the dervishes.

TASAWWUF
The act of devoting oneself to the mystic life and becoming what is known in Islam as a Sufi.

TEKKE
Dervish prayer lodge.

ZIKR (DHIKR)
Reminding oneself, a repetition. "A remembering." Religious service "remembering" Allah by the repetition of His Name. In tasawwuf, the zikr is the most frequent form of prayer, but never replaces the salat. There are three main stages of the experience: those of the tongue, the heart, and of the "inmost being" *(sirr)*.

BIBLIOGRAPHY

ABU BAKR SIRAJ ED-DIN *The Book of Certainty*, New York: Samuel Weiser, 1970

ARASTEH, REZA *Rumi, the Persian, the Sufi*, Tucson, Ariz.: Omen Press, 1972

ARBERRY, A. J. *Discourses of Rumi,* London: John Murray, 1961; New York: Samuel Weiser, 1972 (paper)

_____*Sufism*, London: George Allen and Unwin, 1950; New York: Harper Torchbooks, 1970 (paper)

ARDALAN, N. and L. BAKHTIAR *The Sense of Unity*, Chicago: The University of Chicago Press, 1973

ARNOLD, EDWIN *Pearls of Faith*, London: Trubner and Co., 1886

'ATTAR, FARIDU' D-DIN *The Speech of the Birds*, tr. by Peter Avery, London: The Islamic Texts Society, 1998

_____*Memoirs of Saints*, tr. by Dr. B. Behari, Lahore, Pakistan: Sh. Muhammad Ashraf, 1961

_____*The Conference of the Birds*, tr. by Afkham Darbandi and Dick Davis, New York: Penguin Classics, 1984

BENNETT, JOHN G. *Witness*, London: Hodder and Stoughton, 1962; Tuscon, Ariz.: Omen Press, 1974 (paper)

BIRGE, JOHN KINGSLEY, Ph.D. *The Bektashi Order of Dervishes*, London: Luzac & Co., 1965

BROWN, JOHN P. *The Darvishes*, London: Frank Cass & Co., 1968

BURCKHARDT, TITUS *An Introduction to Sufi Doctrine*, Lahore, Pakistan: Sh. Muhammad Ashraf, 1959

CHITTICK, WILLIAM C., *The Sufi Path of Love*, Albany, N.Y.: State University of New York Press, 1983

_____*Sufism, A Short Introduction,* Oxford: One World, 2000

_____*The Self-Disclosure of God*, Albany, N.Y.: State University of New York Press, 1998

CORBIN, HENRY *Creative Imagination in the Sufism of Ibn 'Arabi,* London: Routledge and Kegan Paul, 1969

DALLAS, IAN *The Book of Strangers*, New York: Pantheon Books, 1972

EATON, GAI, *Islam and the Destiny of Man*, George Allen & Unwin, 1985

_____*Remembering God*, Cambridge: The Islamic Texts Society, 2000

EFLAKI *Account of the Life of Rumi*, with the first book of the Mesnevi, tr. by James W. Redhouse, London: Trubner & Co., 1881

_____*Encyclopedia of Islam*, edited by M. Th. Houtsma, A. J. Wensinck, et al., 4 vols., Leiden, Holland: E.J. Brill, 1911–38

FRIEDLANDER, SHEMS, *Submission, Sayings of the Prophet Muhammad*, New York: Harper & Row, 1977

_____*When You Hear Hoofbeats Think of a Zebra*, New York: Harper & Row, 1987; California: Mazda, 1992

_____*Rumi, The Hidden Treasure*, Louisville, Ky.: Fons Vitae, 1998; Cambridge, Archetype, 2001

AL-GHAZZALI *Classical Persian Literature*, tr. by A. J. Arberry, London:

George Allen and Unwin, 1958

____*Ihya*, tr. by Margaret Smith, in *Al-Ghazzali the Mystic,* London: Luzac & Co., 1944

GILANI, SHAIKH MUHYDDIN ABDUL QADIR *Futuh Al-Ghaib (The Revelations of the Unseen),* tr. by M. Aftabud-din Ahmad, Lahore, Pakistan: Sh. Muhammad Ashraf, 1949

GLASSE, CYRIL, *The Concise Encyclopedia of Islam*, New York: Harper & Row, 1989

GOLPINARLI, DR. ABDULBAKI *Mevlana'dan Sonra Mevlevilik,* Istanbul:1953 (section tr. from the Turkish by Talat Sait Halman)

HAKIM, DR. KHALIFA 'ABDUL *The Metaphysics of Rumi*, Lahore, Pakistan: Institute of Islamic Culture, 1965

IBN 'ARABI *Sufis of Andalusia,* tr. by R. W. J. Austin, London: George Allen and Unwin, 1971

IQBAL, AFZAL *Life and Work of Rumi*, Lahore, Pakistan: Institute of Islamic Culture, 1956

KHALDUN IBN *The Muqaddimah*, tr. by Franz Rosenthal, 3 vols., New York: Pantheon, 1958

KHAN, HAZRAT INAYAT *The Sufi Message*, 12 vols., London: Barrie and Rockliff

KHAN, PIR VILAYAT INAYAT *Toward the One*, New York: Harper and Row, 1974

The Koran, tr. by Abdullah Yusuf Ali, Mushaf Al-Madinah An-Nabawiyah

LEWIS, FRANKLIN D. *Rumi, Past and Present, East and West*, Oxford: One World, 2000

LINGS, MARTIN *A Sufi Saint of the Twentieth Century*, London: George Allen and Unwin, 1961; Los Angeles: University of California Press, 1973 (paper)

____*What is Sufism?*, Berkeley, Calif.: University of California Press, 1975

____*Muhammad*, London: George Allen & Unwin, 1983

MEYEROVITCH, EVA *Themes Mystiques Dans L'Oeuvre de Djalal-Ud-Din Rumi,* Paris: Universite de Paris, 1968

MEYEROVITCH, EVA DE VITRAY, *Rumi and Sufism*, Sausalito, Calif.: Post-Apollo Press, 1987

NASR, SEYYED HOSSEIN *Ikwan Al-Safa, Rasa'il, An Introduction To Islamic Cosmological Doctrines*, Cambridge, Mass.: Belknap Press, 1964

____ed., *Islamic Spirituality,* Vols. 1 & 2, New York: Crossroad, 1991

____*The Heart of Islam*, San Francisco, Calif.:Harper Collins, 2002

NICHOLSON, REYNOLD *A Literary History of the Arabs*, London: Cambridge University Press, 1930

NIZAMI *The Story of Layla and Majnun*, tr. by Dr. R. Gelpke, London: Bruno Cassirer, 1966

PARDOE, JANE *The City of the Sultan*, 2 vols., London: Henry Colburn, 1837

PEARS, SIR EDWIN *Turkey and Its People*, London: Methuen & Co., 1911

RICE, CYPRIAN, O.P. *The Persian Sufis*, London: George Allen and Unwin, 1964

RUMI *Divani Shamsi Tabriz*, tr. by R. A. Nicholson, Cambridge: Cambridge

University Press, 1898; San Francisco: The Rainbow Bridge, 1973 (paper)

____*Mathnawi*, tr. by R. A. Nicholson, London: Luzac & Co., 1925–40

____*Rumi, Poet and Mystic*, tr. by R. A. Nicholson, London: George Allen and Unwin, 1964

____*Signs of the Unseen (Fihi Ma Fihi)*, tr. by W. M. Thackston, Jr., Boston: Shambala,1994

____*Rubaiyat*, tr. into English verse by A. J. Arberry, London: Emery Walker, 1949

SA'DI *The Rose Garden*, tr. by E. B. Eastwick, London: Octagon Press, 1974 (paper)

SCHIMMEL, ANNEMARIE, *Mystical Dimensions of Islam*, Chapel Hill, N.C.: University of North Carolina Press, 1975

____*The Triumphal Sun*, East-West Publications U.K., 1980

____*And Muhammad Is His Messenger*. Chapel Hill, N.C.: University of North Carolina Press, 1985

____*Look! This Is Love,* Boston: Shambhala Publications Inc., 1991

____*I Am Wind, You Are Fire*, Boston: Shambhala Publications Inc., 1992

SCHUON, FRITHJOF *Dimensions of Islam*, tr. by Peter Townsend, London: George Allen & Unwin, 1969

____*Understanding Islam*, tr. by D. M. Matheson, London: George Allen & Unwin, 1963

SHABISTARI, SA'D AL-DIN MAHMUD *The Garden of Mystery,* tr. by E. H. Whinfield, London, 1880

SHAH, IDRIES *The Sufis*, New York: Doubleday & Co., 1964

____*Tales of the Dervishes*, New York: E.P. Dutton, 1970 (paper)

____*The Way of the Sufi,* New York: E.P. Dutton, 1970 (paper)

SINGH, KIRPAL *Naam or Word*, Delhi: Ruhani Satsang, 1972

SMITH, ALBERT *A Month at Constantinople*, London: David Bogue, 1850

SMITH, MARGARET *Readings from the Mystics of Islam*, London: Luzac & Co., 1950

____*Rabi'a the Mystic*, Cambridge: Cambridge University Press, 1928

STAR, JONATHAN tr. *Rumi, In the Arms of the Beloved*, New York: Tarcher/Putnam, 1997

TRIMINGHAM, J. SPENCER *The Sufi Orders in Islam*, London: Oxford University Press, 1971

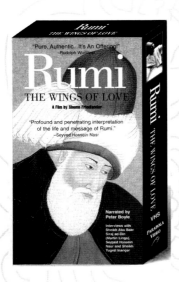

RUMI: THE WINGS OF LOVE
A FILM BY SHEMS FRIEDLANDER

Enter a mystical world rarely seen by outsiders.

Nearly eight centuries after his death, Mevlana Jalalu'ddin Rumi, Sufi master and mystical poet, is ever-present in the whirling ceremony of today's Mevlevi dervishes.

Filmmaker Shems Friedlander was given unprecedented access to document sacred ceremonies; the Halveti zikr, Mevlevi semas, and the Gharib ~~~~~~~~~~~~~~~~~~~~~~~~~~~~ 100 years—were ~~~~~~~~~~~~~~~~~~~~~~~~~~~~~~~ Konya. This unique ~~~~~~~~~~~~~~~~~~~~~~~~~~~~~ levi music and includes ~~~~~~~~~~~~~~~~~~~~~~~~~~~ n Nasr and Martin ~~~~~~~~~~~~~~~~~~~~~~~~~~~ ry of awakening.

Written, produced, and directed by Shems Friedlander
Narrated by Peter Boyle
Edited by Steve Sprung
Music direction by Nezih Uzel

~~~ s the ~~~ g."
~~~ PRA Review

~~~ actful sub-
~~~ mage and

~~~ am Weekly

For orders in North America:

1 VHS cassette, NTSC form ~~~
34 min; color; $24.95 + shi ~~~

Order from Parabola
656 Broadway, New York, ~~~
Phone: 212-505-6200 ext. ~~~
Fax: 212-979-7325
email: orders@parabola.org ~~~
or order online via our sec ~~~
www.parabola.org

~~~ rope and Asia:

~~~ ormat
~~~ + shipping/handling
~~~ er value; worldwide
~~~ % of order value (min ~~~

~~~ books@archetype.uk.con ~~~

~~~ oks Ltd.
~~~ n E9 5LN, UK
~~~ 354
~~~ 821
~~~ ks.com
~~~ downloaded from:
~~~)